EXPLORATIONS IN LOCAL AND

REGIONAL HISTORY

Centre for Regional and Local History, University of Hertfordshire

and

Centre for English Local History, University of Leicester

SERIES EDITORS: KATRINA NAVICKAS AND RICHARD JONES

ASSEMBLING ENCLOSURE

Transformations in the rural landscape
of post-medieval north-east England

BY RONAN O'DONNELL

UNIVERSITY OF HERTFORDSHIRE PRESS

Explorations in Local and Regional History
Volume 7

First published in Great Britain in 2015 by
University of Hertfordshire Press
College Lane
Hatfield
Hertfordshire
AL10 9AB

British Library Cataloguing in Publication Data
A catalogue record for this book is available from the British Library

ISBN 978-1-909291-43-0

Design by Arthouse Publishing Solutions Ltd
Printed in Great Britain by Henry Ling Ltd, Dorchester

Contents

Figures

Abbreviations

CAS   Cumbria Archives Service
DUSC Durham University Special Collections
NRO   Northumberland County Record Office

Acknowledgements

I would like to acknowledge the financial support of the Arts and Humanities Research Council in the completion of the thesis upon which this book is based, and the Aurelius Trust for a grant towards its publication. I am also very grateful to the staff of the Northumberland Record Office and Durham University Special Collections for their help and advice in using their archives, and to the staff of the Northumberland Historic Environment Record, particularly Dr Chris Burgess and Liz Williams. I would also like to thank Dr Paul Harrison for guiding me through the literature surrounding non-representational theory, and Drs David Petts and Richard Jones, who examined the thesis, for their helpful comments. Dr Jones and Dr Katrina Navickas also provided particularly useful comments as the thesis was converted into a book, as did Jane Housham of the University of Hertfordshire Press. I would like to give special thanks to my supervisors, Professor Christopher Gerrard and Dr Sarah Semple, for their help and guidance throughout my doctoral studies. Finally, I would like to thank my wife, Tina, for her patience and support throughout the preparation of both thesis and book.

Series Editors' Preface

Explorations in Local and Regional History continues the series of 'Occasional Papers' of the University of Leicester's Department (now Centre) for English Local History, started in 1952. This succeeding series is published by the University of Hertfordshire Press with the Centre for Regional and Local History Research and the University of Leicester.

Explorations in Local and Regional History has three distinctive aims. First, the series seeks to open up new directions, prompt analysis of new sources and develop innovative methodologies in local and regional history. The series follows the fine tradition set by the universities of Leicester and Hertfordshire in empirical research into communities, place, landscape, demography, and social and economic change from the medieval era to the present day. But it also seeks new ways to reinvigorate the significance of local and regional history in the twenty-first century. Though local and regional history can be bounded physically by geography, it is not bounded by connections and networks that stretch over time and space. Local history drills down to find the meaning of place at all levels, from the micro to the global. We encourage both detailed studies of localities in Britain and Europe as well as comparative and more theoretical approaches.

The second aim of the series is to provide an outlet for mid-length studies in between research articles and full-length books, generally within the range of 40,000 to 60,000 words. Such works are hard to place with existing publishers, so our series offers a space for detailed, yet quicker to read, studies than standard monographs. We encourage innovative work from researchers at the start of their careers as well as from more established scholars.

Third, we hope this series is of interest to both academics and students, but also to researchers outside universities. Local heritage is a vital part of today's society and government: applied local history research enables community building through the commemoration of place, informs policies regarding conservation of both the built and natural environment, and of course helps to promote towns and regions for tourism. This series aims to provide historical context for these uses of heritage.

Richard Jones, University of Leicester
Katrina Navickas, University of Hertfordshire

1

Explaining enclosure and improvement

The period between the end of the Middle Ages and the start of the twentieth century is a very lively one in the history of the British landscape. These centuries were characterised, in large part, by enclosure, the principal process in the creation of the neat hedged or walled landscape with which we are familiar today. Of course, the idea that the landscape was *entirely* created through enclosure has rightly been challenged,[1] but its importance is nevertheless apparent. Alongside and intertwined with enclosure ran a movement dubbed, by both contemporaries and historians, as 'improvement', one of whose defining features was the introduction and development of new agricultural techniques. Other major contemporary changes include the desertion of villages, leaving many rural areas dominated by dispersed farmsteads; the creation of ring-fenced farms; and the conversion of land either from pasture to arable or from arable to pasture. The relationship between these processes is the principal theme of this book. But, for now, we need only note that without them we would live in a very different landscape, both aesthetically and legally.

Dramatic periods of change often lead historians and archaeologists to posit that large-scale social, economic or political forces must have been at play. The development of the post-medieval landscape is no exception. Some have seen the changes as the material reflection of the end of feudalism and the rise of capitalism; this, for instance, was an aspect of Brenner's seminal work. Others, notably Johnson, have argued that the changes were connected with the birth of new worldviews which came with the Renaissance or the Enlightenment. And yet others have linked the developments to changes in the prices of agricultural commodities or capital, a theory which is perhaps most fully developed in the

---

1. E.g. W.G. Hoskins, *The making of the English landscape* (London, 1955).

work of Turner.[2] None of these arguments is directly challenged here, but it will be suggested that, by jumping straight to the large-scale, historians have failed to do justice to the complex realities of landscape change. Here the small-scale is taken as a starting point. These processes, it will be argued, were performed by individual people who lived and worked at the level of villages, townships and farms, not that of nations, continents and worlds. These people were often unconscious of the fact that they were involved in processes such as enclosure or improvement; instead, their actions were more commonly informed by their own specific situation. It is these personal and contingent narratives, explored on the local level but which inform significantly on the large scale, that are examined throughout this book.

Northumberland

These processes will be examined in Northumberland, which provides a good corrective to our understanding of enclosure because in previous work it has often been overlooked. Early work on enclosure focused mainly on the Midlands,[3] creating a strong regional bias in our understanding. Recent research has addressed this to an extent, through studies of the south coast,[4] East Anglia[5] and the north-west,[6] but the north-east remains neglected. In the period under review it was certainly a very different region to those which others have examined. It differed from much of the south of England in having extensive upland wastes exploited through shielings and long-distance droving. These were all present in the north-west, but this region lacked the large landed estates of Northumberland.[7] Northumberland landholding was dominated by a large number of estates of

2.   R. Brenner, 'Agrarian class structure and economic development in pre-industrial Europe', in T.H. Aston and C.H.E. Philpin (eds), *The Brenner debate: agrarian class structure in pre-industrial Europe* (Cambridge, 1987), p. 49; M. Johnson, *An archaeology of capitalism* (Oxford, 1996); M.E. Turner, *English parliamentary enclosure: its historical geography and economic history* (Folkestone, 1980), pp. 106–34.

3.   M.W. Beresford, 'Glebe terriers and open field Leicestershire', *Transactions of the Leicestershire Archaeological and Historical Society*, 24 (1948), pp. 77–126; J. Thirsk, 'Enclosing and engrossing', in J. Thirsk (ed.), *The agrarian history of England and Wales*, Vol. IV (Cambridge, 1967) pp. 200–56.

4.   J. Chapman and S. Seeliger, *Enclosure, environment and landscape* (London, 2001).

5.   T. Williamson, *Sandlands: the Suffolk coast and heaths* (Macclesfield, 2005); S.A. Wittering, *Ecology and enclosure: the effect of enclosure on society, farming and the environment in south Cambridgeshire, 1798–1850* (Oxford, 2013).

6.   I. Whyte, 'Wild, barren and frightful: parliamentary enclosure in an upland county, Westmorland 1767–1890', *Rural History*, 14 (2003), pp. 21–38; I. Whyte, 'The costs of parliamentary enclosure in an upland setting: south and east Cumbria 1760–1860', *Northern History*, 43 (2006), pp. 97–115; E.A. Straughton, *Common grazing in the northern English uplands, 1800–1965: a history of national policy and local practice with special attention to the case of Cumbria* (Lampeter, 2008).

7.   D. Petts and C.M. Gerrard, *Shared visions: the North East Regional Research Framework for the Historic Environment* (Durham, 2006).

more than 3,000 acres.[8] Of these, the most well known were the Alnwick estate of the Percys and the Howick estate of the Greys. In addition to these, the earls of Carlisle held certain lands in Northumberland, although their principal estates were in Yorkshire and Cumberland. The Howick estate, which is of the greatest importance to the present study, consisted of two separate blocks: one near the coast, centred on Howick itself, and another in Tweedside.

During the period under examination Northumberland was mostly rural, but lay immediately to the north of the major port and city of Newcastle-upon-Tyne. The county had four main agricultural regions: the uplands, which were mostly fit for sheep pasture;[9] the coast, which was reasonably fertile grain land; the midland plain, which was also good for grain, although quite heavy in parts;[10] and Tweedside, which was very fine turnip land (Figure 1.1).[11] There appear to have been extensive commons before enclosure in both the uplands and lowlands,[12] while arable land was usually arranged in two or more open fields, akin to a Midland field system.[13] Northumberland's post-medieval agricultural landscapes thus provide a unique and neglected subject for historical research.

In order to address this county in sufficient detail to discover the local people and processes behind enclosure and improvement, five townships have been selected for close analysis: Learmouth, Milfield, Howick, Longhorsley and Elsdon (Figure 1.1). These have been chosen for the availability of the necessary documentary and cartographic resources, as the map regression employed here would be impossible without large chronological ranges of manuscript plans. They represent all four agricultural/landscape regions of the county: Learmouth and Milfield are located in Tweedside; Longhorsley on the central plain; Howick on the coast; and Elsdon in the uplands. They also reflect a range of social conditions: Howick was a closed township, meaning that it was nearly entirely owned by one landlord, who in this case was resident; Elsdon was open, meaning that it was owned by a number of freeholders; Learmouth was closed, but had an absentee landlord; while Longhorsley and Milfield exhibited aspects of both openness and closure. They also represent a range of different estates: Howick, Learmouth and

8. Petts and Gerrard, *Shared visions*.
9. T.I. Colbeck, 'On the agriculture of Northumberland', *Journal of the Royal Agricultural Society of England*, 8 (1847), p. 422.
10. Colbeck, 'Agriculture of Northumberland', p. 422; R.A. Butlin, 'Field systems of Northumberland and Durham', in A.R.H. Baker and R.A. Butlin (eds), *Studies of field systems in the British Isles* (Cambridge, 1973), p. 109.
11. J. Bailey and G. Culley, *A general view of the agriculture of the county of Northumberland* (1797; 2nd edn, London, 1813), p. 4; J. Grey, 'A view of the past and present state of agriculture in Northumberland', *Journal of the Royal Agricultural Society of England*, 2 (1841), p. 156; Butlin, 'Field systems', p. 109.
12. P. Brassley, *The agricultural economy of Northumberland and Durham in the period 1640–1750* (London, 1985), p. 93.
13. Butlin, 'Field systems', p. 111.

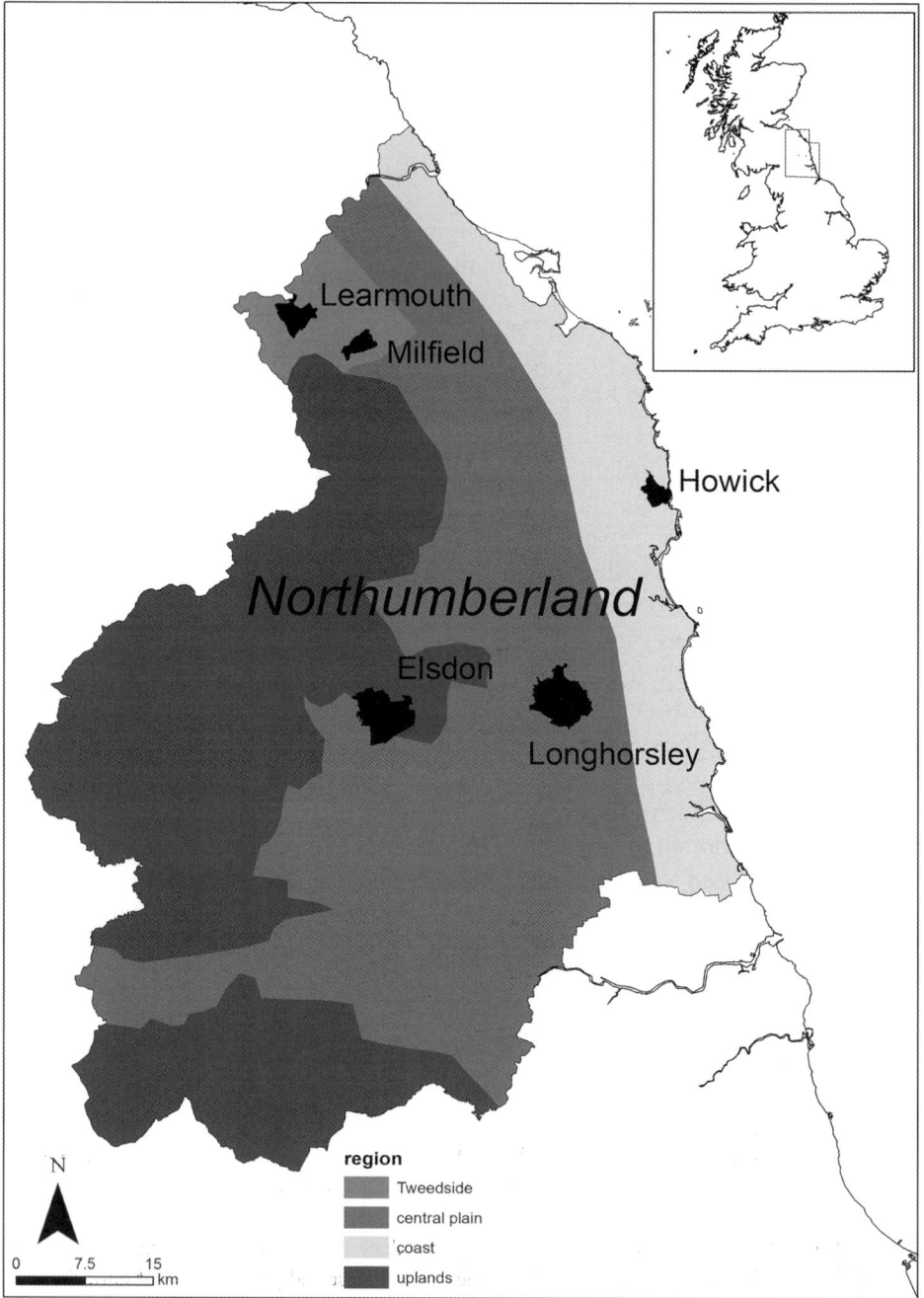

Figure 1.1 The locations of the case study townships. They have been selected in order to represent a wide range of environmental and social conditions, including all four agricultural regions depicted on the map.

part of Milfield all fell within the major Howick estate, while Longhorsley was partially the property of the earls of Carlisle. The remainder of Milfield was owned by the Blakes of Twizel and the Ordes of Nunnikirk.

Learmouth

Learmouth is a township of around 2,500 acres situated in the north-west of the county immediately south of Wark and Cornhill, on the good turnip land of Tweedside. It is currently entirely enclosed and has four clusters of settlement: East and West Learmouth Farms, the Hagg and Tithe Hill. It appears to have been enclosed around 1799 without an act of parliament or formal agreement.[14] The township was originally part of the Barony of Roos and descended with Wark until the late seventeenth century, when Ford, Lord Grey left it to his brother Ralph. In 1705 Ralph died without issue, leaving his Northumberland estate, including Learmouth, to Henry Neville, on the condition that he took the name Grey.[15] When this Henry Grey also died childless, in around 1740, the estate came to Sir Henry Grey of Howick, Baronet. It then remained with the Greys of Howick throughout the eighteenth and nineteenth centuries.[16]

Papers concerning Learmouth from the time of Henry Grey/Neville onward have survived in the estate papers of the earls Grey and lords Howick deposited in Durham University's Special Collection.[17] These include rentals and leases which give details of the tenants, accounts dating mainly to the second half of the nineteenth century, which cover some aspects of improvement, and a pre-enclosure plan of 1793.[18] In addition, the 1843 tithe apportionment and plan[19] and the 1865 Ordnance Survey map provide further detail.[20]

Milfield

Milfield is a township in Tweedside, four miles south-west of Learmouth. It is immediately north of Lanton and appears to have intercommoned with the tenants of that township. Its enclosure and tenurial histories are more complex than those of Learmouth, although the complexity of the former does not entirely result from

14. DUSC GRE/X/P181. In the majority of cases references to manuscript sources, particularly those in the Grey papers and Howard of Naworth papers, refer to a bundle, file or box rather than a specific document. Particular documents may be located by reference to the catalogues of the collections cited below.
15. K.H. Vickers, *A history of Northumberland*, Vol. XI (Newcastle-upon-Tyne, 1922), p. 44.
16. Vickers, *Northumberland*, p. 111.
17. Durham University Library, *Catalogue of the estate records of the Earls Grey* (2009) <http://endure.dur.ac.uk:8080/fedora/get/UkDhU:EADCatalogue.0137/PDF> accessed 11 November 2012.
18. DUSC GRE/X/P276.
19. NRO DT286M Learmouth Tithe Plan.
20. First edition Ordnance Survey map <http://digimap.edina.ac.uk/historicdownloader/downloader;jsessionid=5B687A18BE1F83F10AA3ED16E5A62A5C?execution=e1s1>, accessed 12 March 2012.

that of the latter. Enclosure appears to have occurred in two phases, and in both by formal agreements.

For much of the eighteenth and nineteenth centuries Milfield contained three principal farms: Milfield Demesne, owned by the Ordes of Nunnikirk; Milfield Ninths, owned by the Blakes of Twizel; and Milfield Hill, owned by the Greys of Howick.[21] Unfortunately no documents survive for Milfield Ninths, and very few for Milfield Demesne. The Grey papers are, however, extensive, allowing detailed analysis of Milfield Hill Farm.[22] The earliest plan of the area is of 1777 and shows part of Milfield Hill Farm shortly before the first phase of enclosure.[23] The other two farms were mapped separately in 1821, while the whole township was mapped in 1842 for the Tithe Commutation[24] and 1866 by the Ordnance Survey.[25]

Howick

Howick is on the north Northumberland coast, five miles north-east of Alnwick. The township is the seat of the Greys of Howick, who rose to prominence from the sixteenth century.[26] Edward Grey was the first of the Greys to settle there, after purchasing a tower and some closes in 1593.[27] The estate then passed through the family until in 1750 it came to Henry Grey, who built the hall. He left no issue and so passed the estate to his nephew Charles Grey in 1808. Charles Grey, who later became the second Earl Grey, had a particularly successful career, culminating in his election as prime minister. Charles left the property to his son Henry in 1846. Henry appears to have left the management of the home farm to his brother Frederick Grey, as the estate correspondence is mostly addressed to him.[28] After Henry Grey's death the estate passed to Albert Grey, who owned it at the end of the nineteenth century.

In 1866 Howick contained a small village – which, as will be shown below, is a planned estate village – the hall and park of the Greys, three isolated farmsteads, each with cottages, and several isolated houses. Its enclosure appears to have been early, and was certainly completed by 1759, when a plan was made;[29] as a result, very little can be gleaned from documentary evidence concerning the pre-enclosure landscape. Dating the enclosure more precisely is challenging; there is

21. NRO DT322S.
22. Durham University Library, *Catalogue Earls Grey*.
23. NRO 1356/P26a.
24. NRO DT322S Milfield tithe.
25. First edition Ordnance Survey map <http://digimap.edina.ac.uk/historicdownloader/downloader;jsessionid=5B687A18BE1F83F10AA3ED16E5A62A5C?execution=e1s1>, accessed 12 March 2012.
26. E. Bateson, *A history of Northumberland*, Vol. II (Newcastle-upon-Tyne, 1895), pp. 349–50.
27. DUSC GRE/X/P43.
28. E.g. DUSC GRE/X/P125/10.
29. DUSC GRE/X/P276.

a 1607 enclosure agreement, but this deals only with a small part of the township, and so is part of a longer, more complex enclosure history. It has been suggested that enclosure was complete before 1635.[30]

Longhorsley

Longhorsley is a village in the east of Northumberland, situated on the central plain between Morpeth and Alnwick (Figure 1.1). Its environment is very different from the Tweedside and upland locations of Milfield, Learmouth and Elsdon, being more comparable to the coastal situation of Howick. Also like Howick, enclosure appears to have been completed early, ending with an agreement to enclose the remaining common land, with the exception of a small common in the south and some common grazing on road verges near the village, in 1664.[31]

One of the most striking features of Longhorsley is the complexity of its township boundaries. Certainly by 1866 the area was divided into three townships and a common, a situation which arose following the 1664 enclosure by agreement.[32] The townships were called Bigge's Quarter, Riddle's Quarter and Freeholder's Quarter. Bigge's and Riddle's Quarters were mostly owned by single large landowners, with only one farm in Riddle's Quarter and a few closes in Bigge's Quarter being owned by other people.[33] Both also have detached pieces: in Bigge's Quarter the main ones are called Hayclose and Gibb's Close, and are to the south of Riddle's Quarter; in Riddle's Quarter they are called North and South Bricks, and are to the north of Bigge's Quarter. Freeholder's Quarter was owned by several smaller landowners (Figure 1.2).

From at least the seventeenth century, from when the earliest extant documents come,[34] until 1807, Bigge's Quarter was owned by the earls of Carlisle. The first recorded owner was William Howard, the father of the first earl of Carlisle. The estate appears to have passed from father to son until it was sold in 1807 to Ralph Carr and Charles William Bigge.[35] Bigge and Carr divided the lands between them along the north–south road. The western half, with the exception of closes called Ox Pasture and the addition of 'Further Close' and a moiety of the mill and its lands, went to Carr, and the eastern half and the manorial rights of Freeholder's Quarter went to Bigge. The rest of the manor, the school house and the unenclosed grounds – by this time just the area around the road to the east of

30. R.P. O'Donnell, 'Conflict, agreement and landscape change: methods of enclosure of the northern English countryside', *Journal of Historical Geography*, 30 (2013), pp. 1–13.
31. NRO 358/21/10.
32. First edition Ordnance Survey map 1:10,560 1866 <http://digimap.edina.ac.uk/historicdownloader/downloader;jsessionid=5B687A18BE1F83F10AA3ED16E5A62A5C?execution=e1s1>, accessed 12 March 2012.
33. NRO DT43M, NRO DT391M.
34. The earliest to record Howard ownership is CAS DHN/N12/2.
35. The descent of the manor is recorded in CAS DHN/N/13/11, CAS DHN/N/13/15.

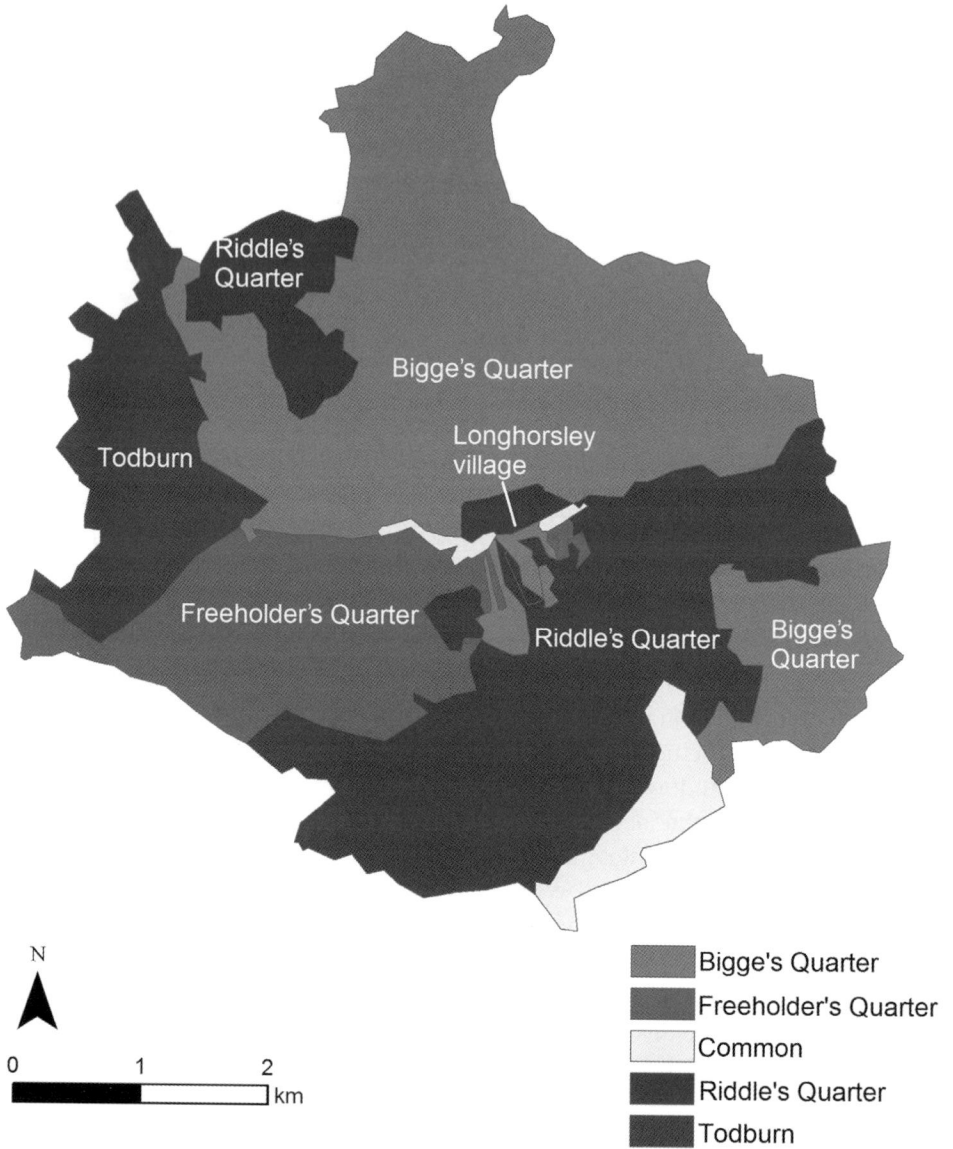

Figure 1.2 Plan of Longhorsley, showing the arrangement of its townships. Note that there are detached pieces of both Riddle's and Bigge's Quarters and that some small pieces of common survive.

the village – were to be held by them as tenants in common.[36] Carr must have left sometime after 1819,[37] as C.W. Bigge is the sole owner of the property in the 1842 tithe survey.[38] The records of this land while under the Howard's ownership are preserved in the Howard of Naworth papers, held by the Cumbria County Council Archives Service.

The descent of Riddle's Quarter is more complicated. It passed by inheritance for the whole period for which records survive but was subject to several failures of male issue.[39] The earliest document which records an owner of Riddle's Quarter is a deed poll of 9 May 1612 in which Isabel Horsley renounced her interest in her father's lands in several places, including Longhorsley.[40] There is then a gap in the records until the 1664 enclosure agreement, which allotted land to Thomas Horsley.[41] He left a will dated 1684 in which he bequeathed his estate to Edward Widdrington, his grandson by one of his daughters, on the condition that he take the name Horsley.[42] Edward Horsley Widdrington left it to his daughter, who married a man called Thomas Riddle.[43] They left it to their son Edward Horsley Widdrington Riddle in 1792. He died intestate and without male issue, so the lands went to his brother Thomas Riddle. Thomas left it to his son Ralph in 1798. Finally, Ralph Riddle left it to his son Thomas Riddle in 1833.[44] Thomas still held most of Riddle's Quarter in 1842.[45] There is no complete set of estate papers for the Horsleys, Widdringtons or Riddles, although isolated documents do survive in the Northumberland County Record Office, including a set of plans dated 1777.[46] These exist in the form of 12 separate plans each showing a different farm, although they appear to have once been joined together. Alongside the tithe plan of 1846 these provide most of the available data on Riddle's Quarter.[47]

At least by 1842 most of the farms in all three quarters were tenanted. The only exceptions, according to the tithe plan, were Muckley Farm in Freeholder's Quarter, which was owned by Robert Clerk, and a close, also in Freeholder's Quarter, which was owned by Patrick Ogg.[48] The house and park at Bigge's Quarter was also owner-occupied, although agricultural land does not appear to

36. CAS DHN/N/13/15.
37. NRO 324.F2/20.
38. NRO DT43M.
39. NRO 358a/33.
40. NRO 358/7/3.
41. NRO 358/21/10.
42. NRO 358a/33.
43. NRO 358a/33.
44. NRO 358a/33.
45. NRO DT391M.
46. NRO 1255/1.
47. NRO DT391M.
48. NRO DT192M.

have been included with this property.[49] There may have been owner-occupied farms either before or after 1842, but the Carlisle rentals show that the farms in Bigge's Quarter were all tenanted up to 1807, while a lease of 1818 survives for Freeholder's Quarter.[50]

Elsdon

Elsdon is situated in the south-west of Northumberland, on the edge of the modern National Park. It differs from other townships studied here in several important respects. First, the number of farms, and thus of landowners and tenants, is much higher than elsewhere, with 88 separate properties listed in the tithe apportionment.[51] This meant that there was a range of landholders of different social groups, from the aristocracy, including the dukes of Northumberland, to those with only a few acres.

Furthermore, the land is much poorer than in any of the other case study townships. It is ranked as Grades 4 and 5 of the Agricultural Land Classification, which are the poorest grades in this national survey.[52] Such poor land was most suited to a mainly pastoral economy, with available records suggesting that much of the township's area was under grass.[53] The wills of tenants at Elsdon often bequeath cows and dairy equipment, suggesting that dairying was significant.[54] This may have discouraged tenants interested in 'improved' farming, as fewer elements of this seem to have been used at Elsdon.

Perhaps because of these differences, Elsdon had a much more irregular enclosure history than Howick, Milfield or Learmouth. Enclosure here happened by two processes. The common was enclosed in 1731 by act of parliament, while the enclosure of the open fields occurred over a much longer period of time, beginning before the 1731 act and being still incomplete by 1945. This process seems to have included both small-scale agreements and piecemeal enclosure.

Elsdon is poorly documented. The earliest plan of the whole township is that which accompanies the 1731 enclosure award.[55] It was mapped again in 1839 for the tithe commutation, and in 1866 by the Ordnance Survey.[56] In addition to

---

49. NRO DT43M.
50. For the tenants of Bigge's Quarter to 1807 see: CAS N/111, CAS N/75, CAS N/112, CAS N/113, CAS N/114, CAS N/115, CAS N/116, CAS N/117, CAS N/101; for the 1818 lease see: NRO 530/17/18.
51. NRO DT164M.
52. Agricultural Land Classification <http://magic.defra.gov.uk/datadoc/metadata.asp?dataset=2>, accessed 15 August 2012.
53. NRO ZBS/25/1, NRO ZHE/14/13.
54. DUSC DPRI/1/1838/K1/1–2, DUSC DPRI/1/1795/H4/1–2, DUSC DPRI/1/1836/A2/1–2.
55. NRO QRD3.
56. NRO DT164M, First edition Ordnance Survey map <http://digimap.edina.ac.uk/historicdownloader/downloader;jsessionid=5B687A18BE1F83F10AA3ED16E5A62A5C?execution=e1s1>, accessed 12 March 2012.

these are several plans of parts of the township mostly dating to the 1830s. There are also several deeds relating to Elsdon in the records of the Morpeth solicitors Brumell and Sample.

Introducing enclosure

These townships will be used to explore five of the most important processes associated with enclosure and 'improvement' – enclosure, farm consolidation, land-use change, settlement dispersal and agricultural improvement – and to examine how they were played out on a local scale. Each of these processes was complex, so, before addressing the Northumbrian evidence, their general features must be outlined.

At its most basic level, enclosure might essentially be defined as the abolition of common rights over particular pieces of land.[57] This was achieved through a variety of means, of which the simplest was unity of possession. Where one person came to own all the holdings with rights over a particular piece of land, usually a township, common rights effectively ceased to exist.[58] This was common from the fifteenth century onwards and was frequently used to turn whole townships over to sheepwalk. Landscape transformation and the eradication of common rights might also be achieved through 'piecemeal enclosure', a process that was ubiquitous from the early modern period onwards but which is probably medieval in origin (Figure 1.3). As the name suggests, large-scale enclosure was, in this instance, achieved through incremental steps. It generally involved a single landowner or tenant purchasing or swapping strips in the open fields in order to consolidate his or her holdings in one place. Assarting, which was common throughout the medieval and early modern periods, is similar to piecemeal enclosure in scale but involves the intake of areas of common waste.[59] Assarting is among the earliest type of enclosure and was common from the thirteenth century onwards.[60] Alternatively, land could be enclosed by agreement between all the rights-holders. Agreements became popular in the seventeenth century, as enclosure began to be used to create mixed farms rather than just pasture (Figure 1.3).[61] Enclosure by agreement was particularly important in Northumberland, as it was used to enclose most of

57. Thirsk, 'Enclosing and engrossing', p. 200.
58. J.A. Yelling, *Common field and enclosure in England 1450–1850* (London, 1977), p. 7. A township is the agricultural territory of a village, over which the members of the village community held rights. In Northumberland they are usually between three and five square kilometres.
59. In this book the terms 'common' (where used as a noun) or 'common grazing' are used to refer to areas over which common grazing rights operated. 'Waste' is used to refer more generally to areas of unimproved pasture, whether or not common rights operated over them. In most cases examined here waste was also common.
60. C. Dyer, 'Conflict in the landscape: the enclosure movement in England, 1220–1349', *Landscape History*, 28 (2006), pp. 21–33.
61. M. Beresford, *The lost villages of England* (1954; 2nd edn, Gloucester, 1983), p. 141.

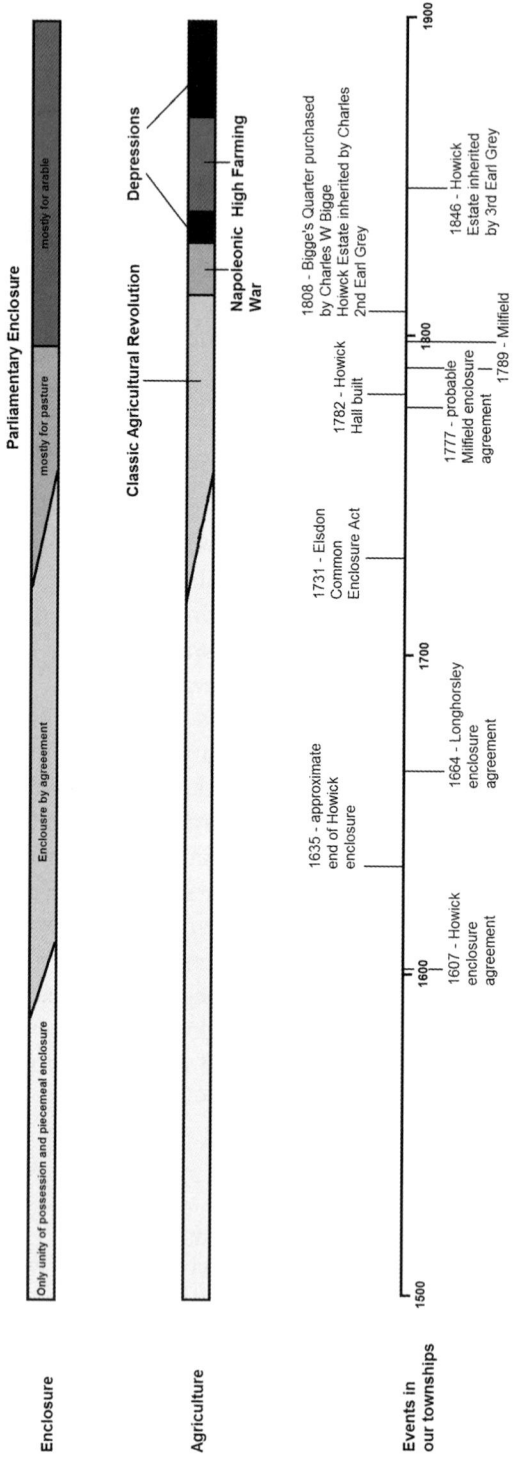

Figure 1.3 A diagram summarising the events of agricultural and enclosure history between AD 1500 and 1900, compared with important events at our five townships. Note that, while distinct phases are marked within enclosure history, piecemeal enclosure continued throughout the period even after the beginning of the enclosure by agreement phase and agreements were used alongside acts of parliament.

the county's open fields during the seventeenth century.[62] In this period enclosure was fuelled by migration into Northumberland as coal production increased, and by the transfer of people from agriculture to industry within the county. This led to increasing tenant prosperity.[63] But it is unlikely that wealth alone would have caused enclosure; landlord pressure was probably also necessary.[64] The landlords, in turn, needed to increase their incomes to fund mortgages. Some were unable to do this and sold their land to businessmen from Newcastle-upon-Tyne, who often took a more professional attitude to their estates.[65]

Finally, enclosure could be achieved by private act of parliament. This method became widespread from around 1760, although many earlier examples exist (Figure 1.3).[66] It grew rapidly in popularity during the Napoleonic Wars, when grain prices were high and interest rates low.[67] Acts of parliament were issued throughout the nineteenth century. In Northumberland most acts were passed to enclose waste rather than the agricultural cores of townships.[68] Earlier types of enclosure did not come to an end as new methods were developed, so assarting and piecemeal enclosure went on alongside parliamentary enclosure during the eighteenth and nineteenth centuries.[69]

In the existing literature the creation of ring-fenced farms is often associated with enclosure, and it is certainly true that, in some cases, their creation may have been a major attraction for eighteenth- and nineteenth-century enclosers.[70] The process is linked to enclosure because the latter often led to the abolition of open-field fallow and post-harvest grazing rights and might include the abolition of open-field divided holdings. Indeed, the grouping of formerly dispersed open-field holdings may well have been the main reason behind many enclosures. However, it must be recognised that there were many instances in which enclosure did not create ring-fenced farms. This is especially true when open fields disappeared gradually through piecemeal enclosure. It was also possible for parliamentary enclosures to award divided holdings where other concerns were more important. Ring-fenced farms were thus not an inevitable outcome of enclosure *per se*, even if their creation required it.

62. Brassley, *Agricultural Economy*, p. 94.
63. Brassley, *Agricultural Economy*, p. 172.
64. Brassley, *Agricultural Economy*, p. 174.
65. Brassley, *Agricultural Economy*; R. Newton, *The Northumberland landscape* (London, 1972), p. 120.
66. W.E. Tate, *A domesday of English enclosure acts and awards* (Reading, 1978); R.J.P. Kain, J. Chapman and R.R. Oliver, *The enclosure maps of England and Wales 1595–1918* (Cambridge, 2004).
67. Turner, *English parliamentary enclosure*, pp. 106–34.
68. Turner, *English parliamentary enclosure*, p. 126; Tate, *Domesday*, pp. 200–203.
69. Chapman and Seeliger, *Enclosure, environment and landscape*; E. Hughes, *North country life in the eighteenth-century: the north-east 1700–1750* (Oxford, 1952), p. 125.
70. G.E. Mingay, *Parliamentary enclosure in England: an introduction to its causes, incidence and impact* (London, 1997), pp. 36–7.

Enclosure is often also associated with changes in land-use patterns. In the Midlands, for instance, it would appear that many fifteenth- and sixteenth-century enclosures were made to convert arable to pasture, but that by the seventeenth century their aim was to create mixed farming systems.[71] Similarly, analysis of the number of enclosure acts per year has suggested that parliamentary enclosure of the period 1760–90 was mostly intended to lay arable land down to pasture.[72] Contrastingly, during the Napoleonic Wars, parliamentary enclosure was often undertaken to allow wastes to be ploughed up for arable.[73] Although farm consolidation and changing land-use patterns might be thought of as integral parts of enclosure, therefore, in reality few enclosures involved both. As this book will demonstrate, their occurrence was contingent upon a large number of local circumstances.

The other processes to be examined in what follows are generally associated with enclosure but not usually thought of as essential elements of it. Settlement dispersal and desertion is a prominent example. Typically it is thought that villages were deserted often as a result of enclosure by unity of possession during the fifteenth and sixteenth centuries.[74] This has traditionally been associated with the desire of landlords to create sheep pastures to take advantage of high wool prices at the start of the early modern period. In Northumberland, however, the route to desertion may have been a little different; it appeared often to have been driven by enclosure and improvement carried out by seventeenth-century landlords who sought to move their farms out of the villages into dispersed farmsteads.[75] This allied process of dispersal without desertion has, however, received very little scholarly attention, rare exceptions being studies of Salisbury Plain, where farmsteads have been shown to have been built on parliamentary enclosure allotments,[76] and Shapwick (Somerset), where a similar process operated in the eighteenth century.[77]

71. Beresford, Lost villages, p. 141.

72. Turner, English parliamentary enclosure.

73. D. Grigg, The agricultural revolution in south Lincolnshire (Cambridge, 1966), pp. 66–81.

74. Beresford, Lost villages.

75. S. Wrathmell, 'Village depopulation in the 17th and 18th centuries: examples from Northumberland', Post-Medieval Archaeology, 14 (1980), pp. 113–26; P.J. Dixon, 'The deserted villages of Northumberland: a settlement history from the twelfth to the nineteenth century', PhD thesis (University of Wales, 1984).

76. G. Brown, 'Post-enclosure farmsteads on Salisbury Plain: a preliminary discussion', in P. Pattison, D. Field and S. Ainsworth (eds), Patterns of the past: essays in landscape archaeology for Christopher Taylor (Oxford, 1999), pp. 121–8.

77. C.M. Gerrard, 'A rural landscape explored: people, settlement and land-use at Shapwick from prehistory to the present day', in C.M. Gerrard with M. Aston (eds), The Shapwick Project, Somerset: a rural landscape explored (Leeds, 2007), p. 1009.

The improvement of husbandry has been interpreted as an indirect result of enclosure.[78] Improvement is itself a very complex phenomenon. It has been used as an umbrella term for a number of farming techniques introduced from the sixteenth century onwards, including the use of lime, legumes, turnips (and other fodder crops), under-draining, convertible husbandry, the seed drill and artificial fertilisers. Agricultural improvement of the post-medieval period also has an accepted chronology (Figure 1.3). Traditionally the period c.1750–1850 is seen as an agricultural revolution in which new techniques were introduced and productivity increased.[79] This included, and was probably partly encouraged by, a boom in grain prices caused by the Napoleonic Wars. The end of these wars caused a depression but prices had picked up again by the mid-nineteenth century (Figure 1.3). From the mid-nineteenth century onwards another revolution, which has come to be known as 'high farming', occurred, in which high inputs of manures such as guano were used to drive up yields and agriculture was increasingly recognised as a scientific practice.[80] Depression hit again in 1873; grain prices dropped and stayed low into the twentieth century (Figure 1.3).

Certain historians challenge the accepted chronology and believe that improvement began in the sixteenth century, stressing the importance of convertible husbandry and water meadows.[81] Some of these writers have suggested that these were responsible for the increase in food production in the post-medieval period.[82] However, many of the improvements introduced in this period may not have been adopted as widely as contemporary authors suggest. This has led to criticism by many who place the revolution in the traditional period of 1750–1850, the period characterised by the use of fodder crops such as turnips to increase manure output which, in turn, allowed fallows to be eliminated.[83] While doubt may be cast on the importance of early improvement for increasing output it is still clear that agricultural innovation was a feature of the entire post-medieval period; consequently, all phases of the agricultural revolution will be examined here.

78. T. Williamson, *The transformation of rural England: farming and the landscape 1700–1870* (Exeter, 2002).

79. R.E. Prothero, *English farming past and present* (1912; 6th edn, London, 1961); M. Overton, *Agricultural revolution in England: the transformation of the agrarian economy 1500–1850* (Cambridge, 1996).

80. J.D. Chambers and G.E. Mingay, *The agricultural revolution 1750–1880* (London, 1966), pp. 62–7; Williamson, *Transformation*, p. 54.

81. E. Kerridge, *The agricultural revolution* (London, 1967); Thirsk, 'Enclosing and engrossing'; J. Thirsk, *Alternative agriculture: a history from the Black Death to the present day* (Oxford, 1997); R.C. Allen, *Enclosure and the yeoman: the agricultural development of the south midlands* (Oxford, 1992).

82. Kerridge, *Agricultural revolution*.

83. Chambers and Mingay, *The agricultural revolution*, pp. 62–7; Williamson, *Transformation*, p. 54.

While 'improvement' may be used as an umbrella term for the group of methods and technologies described above it is also a contemporary term. It was used in eighteenth- and nineteenth-century agricultural books and journals as shorthand for progressive farming. Some historians and archaeologists have suggested that it represented an ideology which made the project of advancing agricultural method a moral priority, since agricultural efficiency was seen as a mark of civilisation.[84]

Northumberland is likely to have had a particularly interesting history of improvement. It was the home of several noted improvers, including the brothers George and Matthew Culley and the father and son George and John Grey of Milfield. During the classical agricultural revolution several contemporary writers praised Northumberland agriculture. John Bailey and George Culley, writing in 1797, thought that the previous 40 years had been particularly good, as did Young, although the latter thought that there was still much work to be done in the uplands.[85] This local interest in improvement is also present during the era of high farming. In 1847 Thomas Colbeck noted that there had been substantial investment in draining and building, and that many advanced tools had been introduced.[86] He also observed that most farms had a threshing machine and steam engine. John Grey, writing in 1841, also thought that agriculture in the county had advanced rapidly.[87] He suggested that the fact that the fertility of the soil was unexhausted, and that there were no inconvenient old enclosures – by which he presumably meant piecemeal enclosures – had helped to advance it. He did, however, think that agriculture was not scientific enough. Certainly, as will be seen, there is abundant evidence that the large estates which dominate Northumberland were strongly involved in both phases of improvement.[88]

Explaining enclosure and improvement

Models which seek to explain enclosure or improvement tend to do one of two things: they either list the benefits of enclosure and improvement and assume that, as a result, enclosure was performed wherever possible; or they identify one or more large-scale causative factors. Mingay's *Parliamentary enclosure in England* is an example of the former.[89] He suggests that enclosure was not always done for agricultural reasons, but that road improvement, tithe commutation, access to minerals and urban development were important objectives. He also hypothesises that enclosure was carried out to introduce improvements which were not

84. S. Tarlow, *The archaeology of improvement in Britain 1750–1850* (Cambridge, 2007).
85. A. Young, *A six months tour through the north of England*, Vol. III (London, 1771), pp. 92–3; Bailey and Culley, *General view*, p. 23.
86. Colbeck, 'Agriculture of Northumberland', p. 424.
87. Grey, 'Past and present state of agriculture', p. 151.
88. Newton, *Northumberland landscape*, p. 120.
89. Mingay, *Parliamentary enclosure in England*, pp. 32–54.

possible in the open fields, but recognises that there were also many additional advantages.[90] Chief among these was the need for a more flexible division between arable and pasture.[91] It is likely that these factors were considered by people involved in particular enclosures. However, on their own they do not offer a full explanation, as each would be desirable at any time. Consequently, they do not explain why enclosure occurred when it did.[92] In answer to this Mingay comments that the growth of markets, changes in transport costs or encroachment on commons may have forced enclosure at particular times.[93]

Several authors have examined the timing of enclosure and improvement, usually by reference to external factors. This means that particular events are understood as the local manifestation of a global phenomenon. A particularly well-understood example of this is the enclosure of Cumbrian commons. When people began to drive stock through Cumberland to southern markets, unsustainable pressure was put on the commons.[94] This resulted from a breach of the principle of 'levancy and couchancy', which was that no commoner should depasture more stock than could be wintered on his or her holding. Conflict resulted and was resolved through enclosure. This example is specific to Cumberland, which had a unique social structure. There are, however, explanations which apply to the entire country. For instance, the removal of obstacles to the free market may have made enclosure preferable to open-field agriculture.[95] Alternatively, Beresford linked rising wool prices to increasing levels of enclosure and thus village desertion.[96] Similarly, several authors have observed correlations between increasing grain prices or falling interest rates and increasing rates of parliamentary enclosure.[97]

A school of archaeology known as post-processualism, which is concerned with the way in which material culture and landscape are understood through the attribution of symbolic 'meanings', has sought new explanations for enclosure and improvement, and offers some serious challenges to economic models. Tarlow, for instance, has pointed out that economic determinism assumes that the people carrying out an enclosure or improvement responded rationally to price movements and were fully aware of market trends.[98] She suggests that this

---

90. Mingay, Parliamentary enclosure in England, pp. 39–41.
91. Mingay, Parliamentary enclosure in England, p. 40.
92. Tarlow, Improvement, p. 40.
93. Mingay, Parliamentary enclosure in England, p. 21.
94. C.E. Searl, 'Customary tenants and the enclosure of the Cumbrian commons', Northern History, 29 (1993), pp. 126–60.
95. D.N. McCloskey, 'English open fields as behaviour towards risk', Research in Economic History, 1 (1976), pp. 124–70.
96. Beresford, Lost villages.
97. Chambers and Mingay, Agricultural revolution; T.S. Ashton, An economic history of England: the eighteenth century (London, 1955); M.E. Turner, Enclosures in Britain 1750–1830 (London, 1984).
98. Tarlow, Improvement, p. 40.

may not have been true, and describes many cases in which enclosure was not economically successful.[99] It is, of course, possible that the people carrying out the enclosure or improvement were misguided. In a similar critique, Johnson suggests that observing an environmental background does not imply a particular cultural response, and that we should not look for strict cause and effect relationships but for looser explanations.[100] These amount to an acknowledgement that correlations between the incidence of enclosure or improvement and external factors do not explain the full extent of local variation.

These authors, therefore, offer alternative models in response to the shortcomings of strictly determinist explanations. Tarlow suggests that improvement was seen as a moral imperative and was linked with ideas of patriotism.[101] She observed that contemporary writers often used the term 'improvement' to cover a wide range of agricultural and non-agricultural activities, and linked it with any type of progress.[102] In the period after the Enlightenment progress was valued as an end in itself, and so improvement became virtuous. It was also considered to be an index of national social advancement, and consequently a patriotic duty.[103] Improvers were thus responding not to a desire for profit or efficiency but to their consciences. Similarly, Johnson proposes that enclosure resulted from a change in the way in which people understood the world.[104] He suggests that the medieval landscape was inscribed with meaning so that the boundaries of open fields represented social relationships. During the eighteenth century, especially during the Enlightenment, this became a much less obvious way to organise the landscape, as the 'social', 'political' and 'economic' began to be understood as separate domains. This led to the creation of landscapes which no longer inscribed social relationships on the ground. These explanations are still problematic, as in essence they have simply replaced the economy with society as the explanatory force and are therefore still at a loss to explain all local variation. Instead of correlating landscape change with price trends, they correlate it with changes in worldview such as the Enlightenment.

Actor-network theory (ANT), part of a wider school called non-representational theory (NRT), offers a way forward. This body of sociological theory was developed primarily as a critique of post-modernism and as an approach to studying scientific method.[105] However, its new approach to the global and the local, in which the global is not seen as hierarchically above the

99.   Tarlow, *Improvement*, pp. 34–66.
100. Johnson, *Archaeology of capitalism*, p. 45.
101. Tarlow, *Improvement*.
102. Tarlow, *Improvement*, p. 35.
103. Tarlow, *Improvement*, p. 35.
104. Johnson, *Capitalism*, pp. 75–6.
105. B. Latour, *We have never been modern* (Cambridge, MA, 1991); J. Law, *Organising modernity* (Oxford, 1993).

local, is of use to us in attempting to understand enclosure.[106] To understand this we might imagine a farmer speaking to his/her neighbours and suggesting enclosing their township. Our imaginary farmer is aware that the price of grain has risen since the beginning of the Napoleonic Wars and views enclosure as a method for increasing output to maximise his/her profits. The farmer is, however, also considering a number of other factors. He/she has several children and is planning to make a will. It is easier to divide a large freehold farm than it is to divide a smallholding with common rights, so an enclosure will assist in this task. In addition, our farmer is embarrassed by the fact that his/her township is using an essentially medieval farming system when neighbouring communities have long since moved on. The price of grain is only one of several reasons in the mind of our farmer as he/she brings up the subject of enclosure. His neighbours all react in slightly different ways, each based on their own desires and expectations, but eventually a consensus is reached to bring an enclosure. While the price of grain is not exceptionally important in our example it is important for national or regional patterns.[107] This is because grain prices can influence many different places while the other motivations we have discussed cannot. In this sense it is global, or at least large-scale, simply because of its better connectivity. It occurs in our example only because our imaginary farmer considered it, but many other farmers are likely to have done the same and so it is transported to many different enclosure situations. In the terms of ANT, we say that it is well connected and that this connectivity makes it global.[108] This means that the global is found within the local.[109] In this instance the farmer has worked as a 'mediator' for the agency of the grain price, and all of the other motivations we discussed as he/she transported them to our situation. Events such as enclosures – or, indeed, our imaginary conversation about enclosure – emerge as these actors are assembled together, and so the way in which this mediation and assemblage occurs is tremendously important.

In ANT all of the things we have discussed – the farmer, his/her family, markets, neighbouring communities, crops, the farm itself, the Napoleonic Wars – are actors. They are considered to be actors purely because they have an effect on the event. They do not therefore require intentionality in order to be actors as they would in post-processual archaeology. They also do not need to *determine* action in order to have an effect, and so the theory does not return to economic

106. J. Law, 'Making a mess with method' (Lancaster, 2003) <http://www.lancs.ac.uk/fass/sociology/research/publications/papers/law-making-a-mess-with-method.pdf>, accessed 30 June 2013; J. Law, 'And if the global were small and non-coherent? Method, complexity and the baroque', *Environment and Planning D: Society and Space*, 22 (2004), pp. 13–26; B. Latour, *Reassembling the social: an introduction to actor-network theory* (2005; pbk edn, Oxford, 2007), pp. 173–90.
107. Turner, *English parliamentary enclosure*, pp. 106–34.
108. Latour, *Reassembling the social*, pp. 190–218.
109. Law, 'And if the global were small and non-coherent'.

determinism. In ANT the assemblage of actors brought into play by mediators forces a specific action, and an event can be said to emerge from the assemblage. This means that actors can be non-human. We have already discussed some non-human agencies. Perhaps the simplest way to understand this is to think of our farmer as gaining some of his/her ideas about enclosure or grain prices from reading a newspaper or journal, allowing the journal to have an effect.

The final important element of ANT is its relational ontology. It considers things to exist only when they act, even if the effect of their action is very small. Our farmer may be sitting in a chair when he/she raises the subject of enclosure with his/her neighbours, and the chair influences his/her body language, takes up space, is seen and so on. None of these effects are very important for our subject but they are still actions of the chair and thus it continues to exist. As we have seen, things act only because of the assemblage they are in and thus they exist only in relation to their assemblage. We have already seen that our farmer acted in particular ways because of his/her relationship to other actors; the precise assemblage of these things caused the farmer to act in a certain way and because objects exist only in their actions then the farmer could be seen as being made up of the other actors. The result of this is that enclosure, or indeed any event or thing, is unique because it emerges from a unique assemblage of actors.[110] The other implication of this idea is that all actors may be disassembled into their components when examined closely. Consequently, any description of an event is necessarily incomplete and thus a final explanation is impossible.

Before we return to our attempts to understand the complexity of the local manifestations of the events, we must explore this complexity. We will do so one process at a time, beginning with enclosure itself.

110. See S. Hinchcliffe, 'Working with multiples: a non-representational approach to environmental issues', in B. Anderson and P. Harrison (eds), *Taking place: non-representational theories and geography* (Farnham, 2010), pp. 303–20. It is actually possible to go further than this and see infinite different events in every action, as each actor in the assemblage of actors may be described in infinite different ways. This results from the fact that each actor, as we have seen, is an assemblage of different actors: for example, our farmer is an assemblage of his or her ideas, body, farm, money, etc. Because each actor may be divided into actors who may also be divided then we may describe each differently simply by looking at the network differently. This is, however, not the main theme of the analysis of this book. See Law, 'And if the global were small and non-coherent'.

2

Abolishing common rights

The five case studies used here each have their own complex enclosure history resulting from the variety of actors involved in each. The histories of the enclosures of each township are complex and contingent.[1] The simplest is that of Milfield. The enclosure of Milfield was achieved in two parts. The common, which encompasses approximately one-third of the township, was enclosed in 1789 by an agreement which allotted land to Francis Blake, Henry Grey, William Orde and the earl of Tankerville.[2] The remainder of the township was enclosed earlier, as it is referred to as 'ancient enclosure' in 1789. It is, however, depicted as unenclosed on a map of 1777, which may in fact be part of an enclosure plan, thus tentatively dating the enclosure to 1777.[3] Few of the other enclosures are so formal. At Learmouth the majority of the township was enclosed in 1799 by unity of possession after it had been engrossed by Anthony Compton of Berwick-upon-Tweed and his descendants. This is revealed in an account of expenditure on hedge planting.[4] The main enclosure was preceded by a very small enclosure by agreement which concerned a small amount of glebe land and which created Tithe Hill Farm (Figure 2.1). Howick was similarly enclosed by unity of possession but much earlier – probably around 1635.[5] This was also preceded by a very small-scale enclosure by

---

1. For more detailed treatment of the narratives of enclosure in each township and the reasons for the use of different types of enclosure see O'Donnell, 'Conflict, agreement and landscape change'.
2. NRO QRD6.
3. NRO 1356/P/26a. See O'Donnell, 'Conflict, agreement and landscape change'.
4. DUSC GRE/X/P181. This document, entitled 'Accounts for new hedges, dikes, ditches at the following: Presson, Downham, Sunnilaws, Learmouth, Learmouth East Field, Wark Common', describes the amount spent on hedge planting at each of these places. It is very likely to represent new enclosure, as it is of the same year as the Wark enclosure award and all the places named have similar amounts spent on them as on Wark Common.
5. O'Donnell, 'Conflict, agreement and landscape change'.

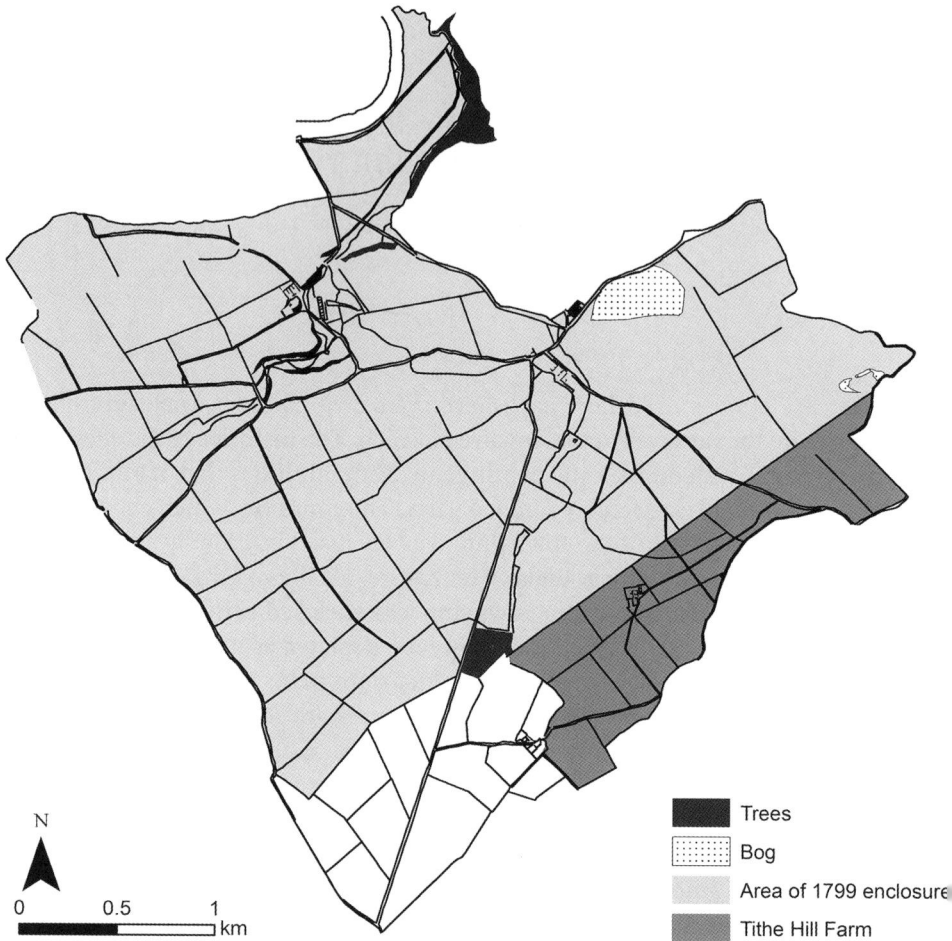

Figure 2.1 The farms in Learmouth, based on the 1843 tithe plan (NRO DT286M). Tithe Hill in the south, coloured dark grey, was created by a small-scale enclosure agreement of the late eighteenth century, which removed the glebe and abolished some tithes.

agreement in 1607.[6] Longhorsley has a yet more complex enclosure history. The forms of field boundaries reveal a certain amount of piecemeal enclosure, at least near the village, while other fields appear to represent assarts (Figure 2.2). An

6.   DUSC GRE/X/P112. This document is an eighteenth-century copy of the seventeenth-century enclosure agreement. It essentially describes the method by which unenclosed land, both arable and waste, was exchanged between Edward Grey and a man called John Craster. The agreement was made by arbitration, the arbitrators deciding that all of Craster's lands be made over to Grey; Craster was then to take lands in lieu in the north of the township, presumably contiguous with Craster's other lands in Craster township.

Figure 2.2 Part of Longhorsley, based on the 1866 Ordnance Survey map. This shows evidence for a number of different types of enclosure, including piecemeal enclosure, revealed by the long, thin, curved fields in the north of the plan (light grey), and assarting, revealed by the 'moor' and 'intake' field names near the common in the south.

enclosure agreement of 1664 completed the enclosure and, as it enclosed a very small area (961 acres 11 perches), may have been the last of several less formal agreements.[7] Finally, Elsdon underwent parliamentary enclosure in 1731.[8] This, however, involved only the common. It appears that some of the remaining land in the township was enclosed by piecemeal enclosure and a number of informal agreements both before and after 1731. It is clear even from this brief discussion that the enclosure histories of the townships under discussion are complex. It would be easy to assign any of the individual events within these histories to a particular external force; for instance, the enclosure of Howick and Longhorsley in the seventeenth century coincides with an increase in the population of the north-east as coal mining expanded. Similarly, the enclosure of Learmouth coincides with rising grain prices. An examination of the detail of each locale, however, reveals these to be very limited accounts and shows that the timing and nature of enclosure was determined by local factors as much as by national and global ones. The same level of complexity and contingency can be seen in the processes by which an enclosure was initiated.

Bringing an enclosure

The most obvious way in which local people and things affected the enclosure histories of particular townships was the making of a decision by a certain person or group of people to make a formal enclosure. This is clear in the 1664 enclosure of Longhorsley. The 1664 agreement finished off a longer process of enclosure which had continued for several decades prior.[9] The agreement itself made the division of the land the responsibility of Sir Thomas Horsley.[10] This may suggest that the enclosure was at the instigation of Thomas Horsley. He was a minor member of the Northumbrian aristocracy and was resident in Longhorsley, so his close connection to the village may have led him to take a greater interest in its improvement, while his wealth allowed him to make changes to the landscape.[11] The enclosure agreement defined a particular process by which the land was to be allotted. Once Horsley had divided the

---

7. NRO 358/21/10. This agreement was made between Charles Earl of Carlisle, Sir Thomas Horsley and a number of freeholders, and appears to have been the final act of enclosure in the township, as it intended 'that there should be a partition and division made as well of the Inne-Grounds as of all and every the Commons and Common of Pasture'. This set out a complex method by which enclosure allotments were to be made, overseen by Sir Thomas Horsley. Interestingly, Horsley's lands were allotted in the Southfield, those of Carlisle in the Northfield and those of the freeholders in the Westfield. These almost certainly represent the three townships into which Longhorsley is now divided and may well be the fields of a three-field system.
8. NRO QRD3.
9. O'Donnell, 'Conflict, agreement and landscape change'.
10. NRO 358/21/10.
11. DUSC DPRI/1/1685/H31/1.

lands, the earl of Carlisle was to choose his share of them, followed by the remaining freeholders. It is interesting that the earl of Carlisle was given precedence over the freeholders, as this may suggest that he had a greater part in the enclosure; however, it may also reflect his different legal status as lord of one of the Longhorsley manors. Alternatively, as he was powerful enough to stop the enclosure, it may have been necessary to allow him precedence in order to persuade him to take part. The freeholders were not without influence, however, as one, called James Ogle, actually opposed the enclosure. His lands were left out of the enclosure until William Ogle (presumably a descendant of James) sold them to a Mr Bulman in 1688.[12] Bulman had been party to the enclosure agreement and went on to enclose his new purchase by exchanging lands with Edward Horsley Widdrington, who was the heir of Sir Thomas Horsley. It is interesting to note that Bulman and Widdrington were related, as Bulman was described as Thomas Horsley's 'cousin' in Horsley's will.[13] It is possible that this relationship facilitated the exchange. Consequently, there is some reason to believe that at Longhorsley particular people had a strong influence on the enclosure itself. There is, however, little direct evidence for this.

At Milfield the evidence for human agency in enclosure is slightly better. Here the earliest evidence for enclosure is a legal opinion dated 1782.[14] This date may be significant, as it is the year in which George Grey became the tenant of Milfield Hill Farm, when the previous tenant, William Mills, surrendered his lease.[15] It may be that George Grey was especially influential in the enclosure of Milfield Common, which seems to be confirmed by a passage in Josephine Butler's book on her family: 'When my grandfather [George Grey] first came to Milfield the plain was still a forest of wild broom. He took his axe, and like a backwood [sic.] settler cut away the broom, and cleared for himself a space on which to begin his farming operations.'[16]

Grey was involved in other enclosures, as he served as a commissioner at Elsdon, and so was clearly interested in enclosure and improvement.[17] It is of course possible that others were influential in promoting the Milfield Common enclosure, and it is not certain that the 1782 document marks the absolute beginning of the enclosure process. Nevertheless, the coincidence of this date with Grey's arrival at Milfield is convincing given Grey's known reputation as an

---

12. NRO 335/21/1.
13. DUSC DPRI/1/1685/H31/1.
14. NRO 1356/M.5. This opinion had been sought by Lord Tankerville, who was the lord of the manor and discussed the legality of some encroachments on the common and his entitlement as lord of the manor in the event of an enclosure. It appears that his position as lord of the manor was in doubt, as his rights as such had not been exercised recently.
15. DUSC GRE/X/P89.
16. J.E. Butler, *Memoir of John Grey of Dilston* (Edinburgh, 1869), p. 10.
17. NRO QRD3.

improver. It seems, then, that George Grey's arrival at Milfield was important in causing the enclosure of the common.

At Learmouth the enclosure occurred as part of an estate-wide policy; the hedge planting account which revealed it also discusses a number of other sites and is thus clearly influenced by the estate or landlord. As we shall see, however, its timing may also imply that the needs of the tenants also played a role. Unity of possession was achieved at Learmouth in 1778 by an agreement to enclose a small amount of glebe. In spite of this, enclosure did not actually happen until 1799.[18] This date is indicated by an account for hedging which lists Learmouth along with Wark Common, Pressen, Donwham and Sunnylaws. These places comprise a section of the Howick estate called Tweedside which was managed separately from the rest of the estate. It appears, then, that the timing of the enclosure of these places, including Learmouth, was the result of estate policy: in short, that the landlord decided to enclose the Tweedside part of the estate. There were good reasons for estate policy to change at this time as Charles Grey (later to be the second Earl Grey) was beginning to take over management of the estate from his elderly uncle.[19] It also coincides with the completion of the Wark Common enclosure. This enclosure was achieved by an act of parliament in which Charles Grey had been instrumental as an MP.[20] It appears, then, that Charles Grey, upon taking over the estate, decided that it would be desirable to enclose the Tweedside part of it and went about doing so, the length of time that this took being partially determined by the time taken to secure an enclosure act for Wark Common. Charles Grey's agency is, however, only part of the picture, as the enclosure also coincides with events in the lives of Ralph Compton, who was tenant of Learmouth, and his brother Fenwick. Learmouth is by far the largest of the farms which were enclosed in 1799, and so it is reasonable to suppose that its tenants had some say in the enclosure, as their failure to give consent may have prevented it. With this in mind it is interesting that Fenwick Compton was admitted to the freedom of Berwick-upon-Tweed in 1799, indicating that he came of age in the same year as the enclosure.[21] This may have been deliberate, as the enclosure was used as an opportunity to divide Learmouth in two to make a farm for Fenwick Compton; indeed, he became the tenant of the new farm upon its creation.[22] It is possible, then, that the Comptons took the opportunity offered by the inheritance of the estate to request the enclosure,

18. DUSC GRE/X/P181. Details of the agreement about the glebe are preserved in a note on a map of 1793 which says that land was allotted to Compton in lieu of glebe and certain tithes (DUSC GRE/X/P276); the 1778 date is provided by the first part of a lease and release by which the tithes and glebe were transferred to Grey and Compton jointly (DUSC GRE/X/P29).
19. E.A. Smith, *Lord Grey 1764–1845* (Oxford, 1990), p. 136.
20. *Journal of the House of Commons* (37 Geo III 22 May), 53, p. 594.
21. Vickers, *Northumberland*, p. 30.
22. DUSC GRE/X/P78.

or alternatively that Grey made the enclosure attractive to them by allowing it to become a solution to their need to provide for Fenwick. This reminds us that while documents regarding enclosure are often silent concerning the tenantry they still may have had a role.

The act for the enclosure of Elsdon Common includes a list of 32 signatories of the petition made to parliament as the first part of bringing a private bill. Little is known of most of these people. However, certain details can be determined from a careful reading of the Enclosure Award, as 22 received allotments.[23] Taking the size of the allotment as a rough proxy for the size of the holding, it can be seen that these 22 included most of the large landowners; nine received over 100 acres, in comparison with only two allotments of this size to people who were either not named in the award or were not petitioners. Despite this, some smaller landowners are present, such as Thomas Hedley, who received only 21 acres and 2 roods, or Edward Hall, who received 22 acres and 32 perches. Ten of the other petitioners are not mentioned in the award. This is either because they received allotments for which no landowner is named in the award, or because they had died or left the township between the passing of the act in 1729 and the making of the award in 1731. Biographical details are known for only one person involved, Jeremiah Bayles. He was not actually a landowner at either the time of the act or the time of the award. On 25 October 1725 he had married Catherine Elsdon,[24] who was entitled to Low Mote Farm by her late father's will, but only in the event of her mother's death.[25] As events actually transpired Jeremiah Bayles never possessed this farm, as he died in 1755, predeceasing Catherine's mother. The land ultimately went to Catherine's half-brother Alexander Hall.[26] In this case Jeremiah Bayles petitioned for the enclosure in the expectation that it would add to holdings that he would come to possess in the future, or in the knowledge that his wife would in any event. Consequently, the enclosure of Elsdon suggests that the wealthiest members of the community may have been more in favour of parliamentary enclosure of the common, although they were certainly not alone in this. The case of Jeremiah Bayles also demonstrates some of the complexity of the

---

23. NRO QRD3.
24. T. Stephens (ed.), *The register of baptisms, marriages and burials solemnized in the ancient parish in the ancient parish church of Elsdon, in the county of Northumberland* (Newcastle-upon-Tyne, 1903), p. 103.
25. NRO ZBS/26/2.
26. NRO ZBS/26/2. This story is described in a bundle of deeds. One of 1729 recites the relationships between the different characters, but is otherwise formulaic, as it is part of a final concord. Later in the deed bundle a 1755 lease and release then actually conveys the lands to Alexander Hall after the deaths of his mother Elizabeth Hall and his half-sister Catherine Bayles, who were each to have half of the land during their lives. All of this was necessary because Catherine's father had left his real estate to Elizabeth Hall 'while she remained his widow', meaning that it passed to Catherine on her remarriage to Alexander Hall's father, leaving any of Elizabeth's children with her second husband without an inheritance.

personal motivations behind enclosure.

The discussion above largely deals with formal enclosures, those brought about by act of parliament or agreement. However, informal enclosure was also significant in all the townships examined.[27] It is much more difficult to discuss the forces which brought about these enclosures as they are by definition undocumented. It is therefore possible that they were used by less wealthy people than those discussed above, allowing the possibility that the predominance of the wealthy in this discussion may not represent a greater interest in enclosure among the elite.

The course of enclosure

We are interested not only in why enclosure happened but in what influenced the ways in which it occurred in each different instance, as there are so many forces at work in each case. This provides a good opportunity to look beyond what people intended to occur in each enclosure event.

Unintentional outcomes

The unintentional outcomes of the actions of the people involved in each enclosure will be considered first. This phenomenon is particularly clear at Milfield, as this enclosure was the subject of two conflicts.

The legal opinions mentioned above concerned the right of Lord Tankerville to the common as lord of the manor and the legality of some encroachments.[28] One opinion was that the earl was in fact the lord of the manor and that the encroachments were illegal, whereas the other suggested that the soil was owned by the commoners and that the enclosures were therefore legal.[29]

Further conflict emerged following the enclosure. A man called Thomas Lowry approached William Orde, who had received a share of the common, demanding 100 guineas on the grounds that he had not been awarded land. He clearly felt that he was entitled to part of Orde's allotment.[30] To resolve this Orde wrote to one of the enclosure commissioners, in April 1790, asking 'the Commissioners to get me out of that unpleasant difficulty as well as they can either by making out & setting off the Publick House allotment from my share of the Common', as he was unwilling to pay Lowry, who could not provide any proof of his entitlement to the land.[31] It is likely that potential for conflict was created by the uncertainty regarding the lordship of the manor.

These two episodes demonstrate the way in which the process of enclosure followed a particular course as a result of conflict between different stakeholders

27. O'Donnell, 'Conflict, agreement and landscape change'.
28. NRO 1356/M.5.
29. NRO 1356/M.5.
30. NRO ZCU/16.
31. NRO ZCU/16.

which cannot be said to be the intention of either party. These incidents do, however, also involve some things besides people, particularly the legal status of the common itself.

The land and its history

The land itself plays an important role in the course of enclosure, showing that the work of people is only one aspect of each enclosure event. A particularly clear example of this is the presence of glebe land, which often required a more formal type of enclosure or prevented enclosure altogether. At Learmouth an agreement of 1778 enclosed a small amount of glebe and some land in lieu of tithes. The agreement involved, firstly, the purchase of the glebe and tithes by Henry Grey and Ralph Compton and, secondly, the grant of a small piece of land to Ralph Compton, almost certainly that which later formed Tithe Hill Farm, in exchange for his share. This ultimately paved the way for the 1799 enclosure of the rest of the township by the uniting of all the land under one tenant and one owner. As the glebe was the only land enclosed in this agreement it is likely that the agreement was used because the glebe presented specific legal difficulties. At Elsdon glebe appears to have prevented or at least slowed piecemeal enclosure. To the east of Elsdon village an area of open field appears to have remained unenclosed up to the twentieth century (Figure 2.3). On the Ordnance Survey map it appears as an entirely open area, whereas the tithe plan shows ownership boundaries within it, suggesting that it was unenclosed, as its property boundaries were not marked by physical fences. Some of the strips in this area are glebe land and it may be that it was these that prevented the piecemeal enclosure of the whole area. Indeed, a man called Mr Gow attempted and failed to enclose some of the glebe land towards the end of the nineteenth century. He purchased a strip of land from the duke of Northumberland around 1874, next to a strip of land belonging to Alwinton glebe.[32] He then bid successfully for the Alwinton glebe strip in an auction later that year.[33] It appears that the sale was prevented, probably by the legal difficulties in alienating glebe, as the strip appears in an 1895 glebe terrier.[34] These strips had previously been joined in practice, as one John Davidson had both sold the former strip to the duke of Northumberland and been the tenant of the rector of Alwinton.[35]

The number of freeholders involved, which essentially amounts to how open the township in question was, is also a very significant factor. Some of the most formal enclosures occurred in the most open parishes, so, whereas Learmouth and Howick were largely enclosed informally, Elsdon and Wark Commons, on which

32. NRO ZHE/14/3.
33. NRO ZHE/14/3.
34. NRO DN/E/9/1/103.
35. NRO DT164M.

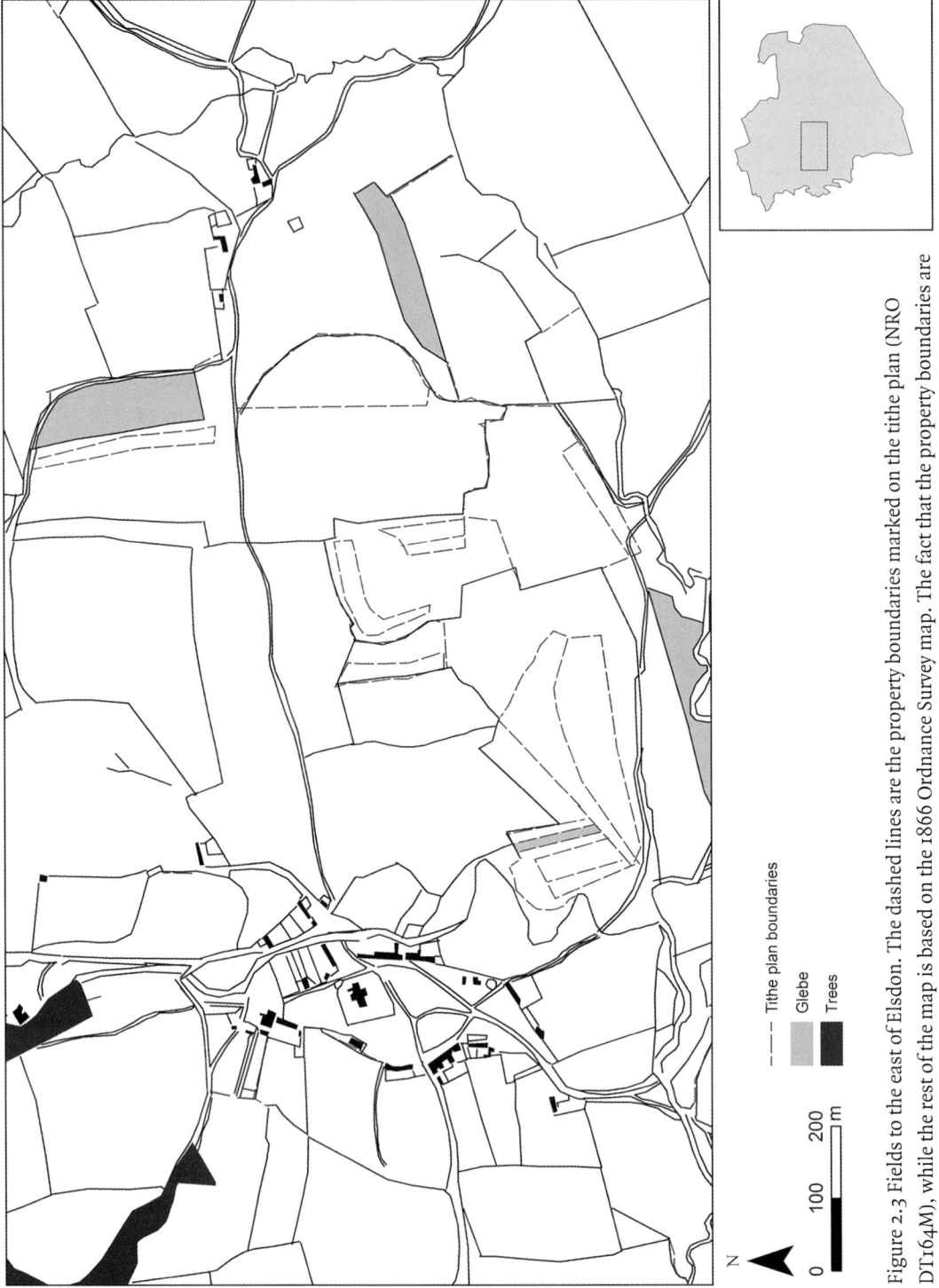

Figure 2.3 Fields to the east of Elsdon. The dashed lines are the property boundaries marked on the tithe plan (NRO DT164M), while the rest of the map is based on the 1866 Ordnance Survey map. The fact that the property boundaries are not marked by any physical boundaries, as depicted on the Ordnance Survey map, suggests that the area was unenclosed.

Tithe plan boundaries
Glebe
Trees

N

0   100   200
m

very many people held grazing rights, required acts of parliament. Similarly, where open lands were intercommoned between several townships, as at Milfield, Wark and Elsdon, they were generally enclosed in a formal manner.[36] The presence of glebe and the 'openness' of the township are quite obvious and indeed common factors, although local in their specific details. However, there are more unusual local factors which also have a major effect on the process of enclosure.

A more unusual case of the influence of the land itself on the course of enclosure appears in the case of Wark Common. Here an act of parliament was used in order to enclose the common.[37] It is likely that this decision was reached partly as a result of the complications offered by the number of proprietors who held rights to the common. However, the fact that the land was part of the 'Debatable Ground' – meaning that it was not clear whether it formed part of England or Scotland – may also have been a problem.[38] The implication of the situation was that by taking land that was intercommoned between English and Scottish townships and dividing it between these townships the enclosure of Wark Common effectively created part of the border.

Similarly, specific needs were catered for by the enclosure agreement at Howick. This agreement was made in 1607 and dealt with only a very small amount of land in the north of the township. The agreement was needed because unenclosed land owned by John Craster was preventing Henry Grey from gaining unity of possession at Howick. It is unlikely that Craster wanted to sell his lands, as they were part of a larger farm, most of which was in Craster township, to the north of Howick.[39] Grey did not need the lands as such, and only needed to separate them from his other unenclosed lands. As an exchange of lands is a relatively unusual occurrence a formal process was required for it. Thus, we see that unexpected actors can have an effect on the process of enclosure alongside the familiar, if local, influences.

Understanding local enclosures

The discussion above has shown that often quite local and unexpected circumstances could have as much effect on the course of enclosure as large-scale factors such as grain prices. The inheritance of the Howick estate by Charles Grey, which triggered the enclosure of the Tweedside area, is a good example, as is the effect of John Craster's and Henry Grey's respective needs at Howick. We have seen, too, that people were not the only influences on each enclosure event, as, for

36. For a detailed discussion of both these factors see O'Donnell, 'Conflict, agreement and landscape change'.
37. NRO QRA36/1.
38. It is marked as such on a map of Northumberland of 1793. J. Cary, *New maps of England and Wales with part of Scotland* (London, 1793).
39. NRO DT211S. This Tithe Plan shows a large farm in Craster in the possession of John Craster's descendants.

instance, the presence of glebe land in a township could be a barrier to enclosure at certain times. We have also seen how people were able to influence circumstances through their relationships to other factors. For instance, the earl of Tankerville was able to oppose enclosure because of his wealth, while George Grey was probably particularly interested in having a formal enclosure at Milfield because he subscribed to a particular set of beliefs regarding agricultural improvement and was part of the intellectual improvement movement.

It is important to remember that each person who decided on a particular approach to enclosure worked from their own knowledge and experience, and so some would be more pedantic about the legality of the procedure than others. Each would also have had different financial means, so some could not afford a complex legal procedure while others could. Thus, the context of each particular enclosure event, the number of landowners, their wealth and status, their knowledge of enclosure, the type of land to be enclosed and the details of its tenure are all highly significant to the way in which the process actually played out. Consequently, we should not think of these people and things as working in isolation, but should see the unique events of each enclosure as emerging from a particular set of circumstances. This concept will be explored below in relation to the remaining types of landscape change to be discussed.

3

Consolidating farms

The creation of ring-fenced farms is an important, though largely unacknowledged, development in the post-medieval landscape. It is perhaps unrecognised because of its minimal impact on the physical landscape and the greater attention paid to more glamorous improvements such as new rotations and machines or improved breeds of livestock. It was, however, recognised as important by several contemporary authors.[1] A number of studies which mention farm consolidation incidentally to their primary subjects suggest that it was fairly common during the post-medieval period. For instance, sixteenth-century peasants in Wigston Magna commonly consolidated open-field strips and similar evidence was found at Shapwick.[2] In later periods, planned reorganisation of the seventeenth- and eighteenth-century landscape formed ring-fenced holdings.[3] Ring-fenced farms certainly had their advantages, which may have been important motives for some enclosures.[4] For instance, they would have allowed under-draining, which would have been near-impossible on non-ring-fenced farms.[5] Such advantages do not, however, demonstrate why the popularity of ring-fenced holdings increased during the post-medieval period. Extra-economic motivations may also be important, as the consolidation of estates by the aristocracy between 1640 and 1750 was for personal satisfaction as much as for easy management.[6] This, of course, refers to the consolidation of land which was mostly held by leasehold tenants and so is not, strictly, the creation of ring-fenced farms. However, as will be seen below, such engrossing could contribute to the formation of ring-fenced farms.

1. J.M. Wilson, *The rural cyclopedia*, Vol. IV (London, 1849), p. 222; W. Marshall, *On the landed property of England* (London, 1804), p. 130.
2. W.G. Hoskins, *The midland peasant: the economic and social history of a Leicestershire village* (1957; 2nd edn, London, 1965), pp. 232–4; Gerrard, 'A rural landscape explored', p. 1009.
3. R. Moore-Colyer, 'Land and people in Northamptonshire: Great Oakley, c.1750–1850', *Agricultural History Review*, 45 (1997), pp. 149–64; Williamson, *Sandlands*, pp. 91–3.
4. Mingay, *Parliamentary enclosure in England*, pp. 36–7.
5. Williamson, *Transformation*, p. 14.
6. C. Clay, 'Landlords and estate management in England', in J. Thirsk (ed.), *The agrarian history of England and Wales*, Vol. V (Cambridge, 1985), pp. 178–9.

Many writers assume that enclosure was the principal process by which farms became more consolidated, and certainly the most detailed discussions of the phenomenon focus on enclosure.[7] While enclosure was certainly important it has been shown elsewhere that the pre- and post-enclosure processes are just as significant, despite rarely being discussed in detail.[8] The following discussion will focus on these poorly understood processes and show them to be as contingent upon local circumstances as the previous chapter showed enclosure itself to be. In some cases it is also possible to show that enclosures led to ring-fenced farms only through the precise combination of local circumstances, although in practice the nature of the documentation makes this more difficult to assess.

The importance of tenants

In contrast to the apparent importance of landlords revealed by other researchers,[9] our townships often reveal the great importance of tenants in creating ring-fenced farms. Learmouth is a particularly clear example. Here a large ring-fenced farm encompassing almost the entire township was created by 1733. This was mostly the work of tenants, although the landlord would at least have been able to stop it and so clearly did not object. The process had begun before 1708, when the earliest surviving record was written.[10] This document is a rental which shows that the farmland in Learmouth was occupied as six farms by John Hall, John and William Crawford (who held one farm as partners), Widow Crawford, Lionel Bolton and Ralph Archibald. John Hall held two separate farms and so had already engrossed land. In 1712 John and William Crawford's and Lionel Bolton's farms were also engrossed by a man called Thomas Gregson. The lease of these farms describes them as 'those six ffarmes com[m]only called the West side of Learmouth',[11] suggesting that earlier engrossment had occurred as well. In 1719 one Anthony Compton, who was an alderman of Berwick-upon-Tweed, became the tenant of a farm called Hurch Law and Mill Land. This is probably the farm of either Widow Crawford or John Hall, as it has a similar rent.[12] On 11 June 1724 he added a farm called Cornhillhaugh and Learmouth, which was probably the other farm of John

7.   Yelling, Common field and enclosure, pp. 120–45.
8.   R.P. O'Donnell, 'The creation of ring-fence farms: some observations from Northumberland', Agricultural History Review, 63 (2015), pp. 39–59.
9.   E.g. Moore-Colyer, 'Land and people'.
10. DUSC GRE/X/P80. This rental gives the rent owed by each farm and the amount received, and calculates from these the arrears of each tenant. It therefore provides a list of all the farmers on the Howick Estate and some indication of the size of their holding. It was created in order to report the estate's finances to Grey and as a record for future reference. It is more substantial than later rentals, as it is several sheets of paper bound in parchment.
11. DUSC GRE/X/P72.
12. DUSC GRE/X/P73.

Hall, again because it has the same rent.[13] In 1733 Thomas Gregson surrendered his lease and Anthony Compton became the tenant of the last remaining leasehold farm in Learmouth.[14] This left only some glebe land to be engrossed. Without knowing where any of these farms were in practice it is difficult to know to what extent each element of the process caused consolidation, and it is possible that some of these engrossments did not actually cause consolidation. However, the ultimate outcome of the process of engrossment was a near-ring-fenced farm. The final step of the process occurred after Anthony Compton's death in 1755, when his nephew, Ralph Compton, the owner of Learmouth, Henry Grey, and the owners of the glebe made an agreement to enclose the glebe. This created a small ring-fenced farm in the south of the township and left the remainder in the sole occupation of Ralph Compton.

It is important to recognise that Learmouth's consolidation was not purely the agency of Anthony Compton. He depended firstly on his wealth, which would have allowed him to stock the farms and convince the landlord that he would not fall into arrears. It is possible that the greater economic power of Compton was what prevented other tenants, such as Hall and Gregson, from carrying out similar engrossment. Compton also depended on being in a position of power, as he was the land agent at the beginning of the process, which would have given him personal access to the landlord as well as some control over who was able to take leases. Finally, and most significantly, Compton's engrossment depended on earlier engrossment, which reduced the amount of work he had to do, and upon the later work of his descendants.

Tenants were similarly important at Bigge's Quarter, Longhorsley. Here the process by which ring-fenced farms came into existence can be reconstructed through the comparison of a plan of 1719, which shows a very fragmented pattern of occupation, and a 1773 plan, which shows ring-fenced farms, alongside data from the rentals of the Howard estate, which owned Bigge's Quarter (Figure 3.1). The best example is found in the eastern part of the township. In 1740 William Grey, William Bell and Margaret Leighton held farms in this area. Unfortunately it is not possible to determine exactly which pieces of land they owned, as the book accompanying the 1719 plan is missing. The 1719 plan appears to depict a fragmented pattern of land occupation in this area, while the 1773 plan shows ring-fenced holdings. In 1740 one Thomas Pinkney took the lease of the farms of William Bell and William Grey. At the same time George Leighton inherited Widow Leighton's farm. This appears to have provided an opportunity to rearrange the boundaries in this area and to create the east–west boundary between these farms. Thomas Pinkney must have been unsuccessful in his farm, as he left in 1741. His farm was divided into three between Ralph Carnaby, Henry Young, and

13. DUCS GRE/X/P73.
14. DUSC GRE/X/P74.

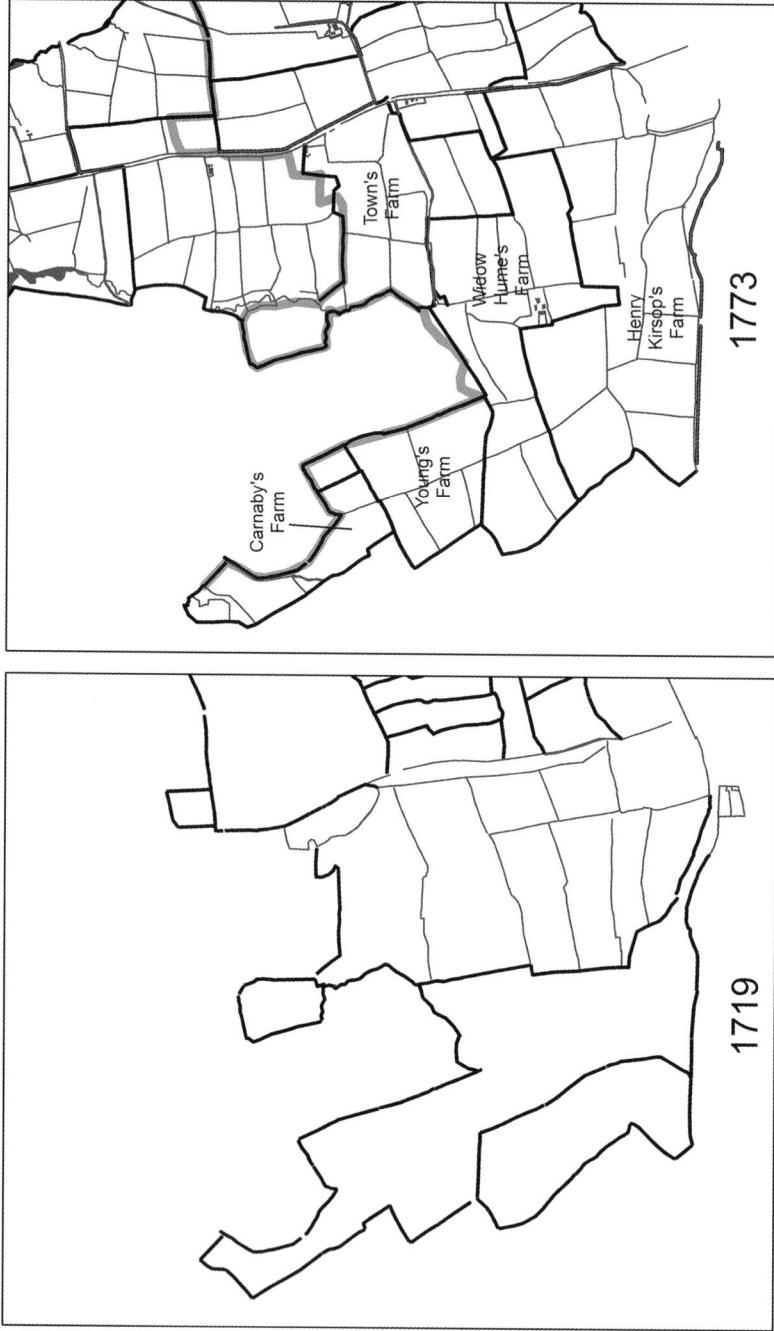

Figure 3.1 The eastern half of Bigge's Quarter in 1719 and 1773, based on DUSC HNP1967/Lambert Plans fos 6v–6d and DUSC N190/97, showing farm boundaries in black. Between these years ring-fenced farms were created through a long sequence of events involving largely tenant agency.

1773

Carnaby's Farm

Young's Farm

Town's Farm

Widow Hume's Farm

Henry Kirsop's Farm

1719

Farm boundaries

Edge of 1719 plan

N

0   0.25   0.5
km

Thomas Hume and Edward Towns, who held the majority of the land as partners. This created most of the boundaries present on the 1773 plan. The remaining boundary was created when Town and Hume dissolved their partnership in 1743. This episode demonstrates the way in which the 1773 pattern of boundaries emerged from the combination of tenants, parcels of land and events. The outcome was contingent upon many chance events, such as the coincidence of the dates of George Leighton's inheritance and Thomas Pinkney's arrival. Similarly, the process depended on Thomas Pinkney's ambition to create a large farm and his subsequent failure.

Landlords

Despite the clear importance of the tenants in the examples described above, landlords are also significant, as any case of consolidation by tenants would have required the landlord to grant two leases to one tenant. This, of course, may have been in a landlord's interest, as he or she may have considered consolidation an improvement and would have found dealing with one tenant easier than dealing with two, particularly if the consolidating tenant were a reliable one.

A clear case of land being consolidated by a landowner occurred at Howick during the seventeenth and eighteenth centuries. The process seems to have begun around 1593, when Edward Grey of Morpeth bought a tower and three acres of meadow from his brothers Roger and Arthur Grey of Chillingham, although it is possible that there were earlier, undocumented purchases.[15] Edward Grey continued to purchase land from other Howick landowners, particularly from the Herrings, who had previously been the principal landowners in the township. Edward Grey bought Green End and Tower Farmholds from Robert Herring in 1596,[16] the mill from William Herring in 1601[17] and a farmhold from Jeffrey Herring in 1603.[18] He also bought holdings from Henry and Elizabeth Swinnow in 1607, and from Cuthbert Lockewood in 1623.[19] Other freeholders are mentioned in a 1607 enclosure agreement and so Grey must have made other undocumented purchases in order to gain sole ownership of Howick (with the exception of a small enclosed freehold in the north of the township) before 1759. This process clearly depended strongly on Edward Grey and his ability to purchase land at Howick. However, it is likely that he chose Howick in preference to other townships because he was able to purchase the tower and meadow easily from his brothers and perhaps was already familiar with the site. Engrossment was also aided by the decline of the Herring family, who sold the majority of the land to Grey.[20] Chance events in the lives of the

15. DUSC GRE/X/P43.
16. DUSC GRE/X/P43.
17. DUSC GRE/X/P43.
18. DUSC GRE/X/P43.
19. DUSC GRE/X/P43.
20. Bateson, *Northumberland*, Vol. II, p. 349.

other freeholders also played a part, as Cuthbert Lockewood sold his farm shortly after inheriting it, perhaps because he was less interested in farming than his father and so liquidated his inheritance as soon as he could.

By achieving unity of possession, Edward Grey created a situation in which permanent ring-fenced farms could arise. The unity of possession was not in itself sufficient for the creation of ring-fenced farms, however, because Edward Grey may well have let the land to tenants as dispersed holdings, and the actions of tenants appear to have been required to finally create ring-fenced holdings. This is revealed by a series of leases dated between 1712 and 1728.[21] These documents name several farms: for example, one of the 1712 leases lets Southfield Farm to Reynold Spoor, while another lets Pasture Farm to William Baxter and Ralph Dixon.[22] There is no evidence as to whether these farms were ring-fenced or not. These leases do, however, mention some closes which appear to have been let separately from the farms themselves. In 1712 two leases were made out to Alexander Young which related to closes called Low Flatt, North Moor, High Flatt, Butterlaw and Pilferlands, in addition to two farms called Lowfield Farm and South Farm.[23] At the same time a close called The Heugh was let to Alexander Marshall.[24] In 1717 Butterlaw, High Flatt, Pilferlands and South Farm were let to Thomas Nesbitt, along with two closes called High Damms and Black Law, which were not named in any 1712 lease.[25] In 1722 Alexander Marshall, who probably still held The Heugh, took a lease of property called the two Flatts and East Farm.[26] Finally, in 1728, Thomas Neal took a lease of The Heugh and the two Flatts.[27] It is clear, then, that the closes could be moved quite freely between different farms. It is also possible that the seeming disappearance of some of the earliest farms and the appearance of new farms and closes in later leases may represent the breaking-up of old farms and the redistribution of closes to form new farms. This implies that, rather than being let as fixed ring-fenced farms, the land at Howick was treated more as a series of separate closes, the consolidation of which was left to the tenants. This situation seems to have pertained until a gap in the series of leases after 1728. Leases are available again only from 1772 onwards, although as the tenants of these leases are named in rentals from 1766 they may represent an earlier situation.[28] The 1772 leases name only three farms, specifically Redstead, Pasture House and Sea Houses, and do not name any closes.[29] Sea Houses is

21. DUSC GRE/X/P72, DUSC GRE/X/P73.
22. DUSC GRE/X/P72, DUSC GRE/X/P72.
23. DUSC GRE/X/P72, DUSC GRE/X/P72.
24. DUSC GRE/X/P72.
25. DUSC GRE/X/P72.
26. DUSC GRE/X/P72.
27. DUSC GRE/X/P73.
28. DUSC GRE/X/P81.
29. DUSC GRE/X/P76.

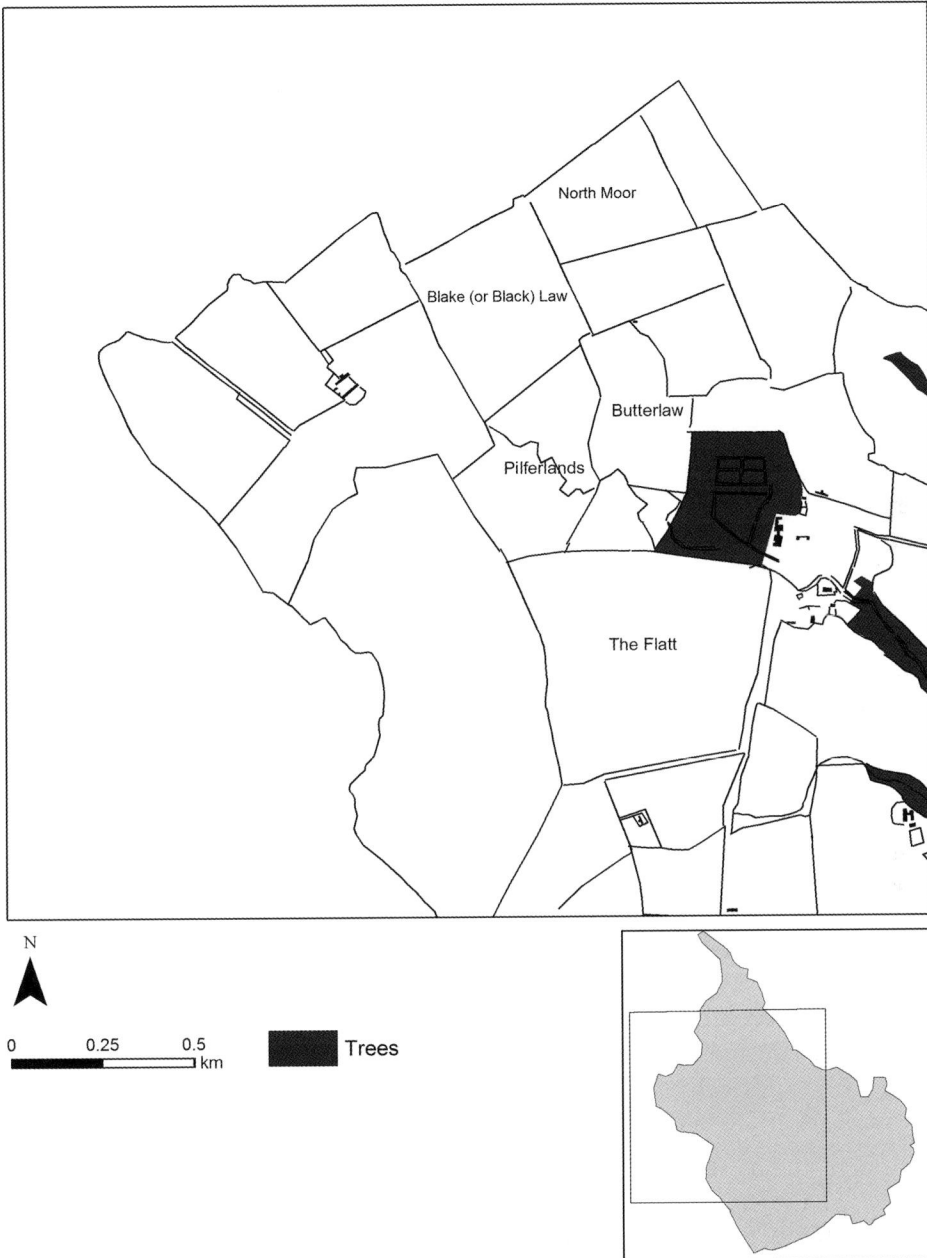

Figure 3.2 Fields mentioned in eighteenth-century leases of Howick. The fields recorded in the same leases are often in the same area, perhaps suggesting that they were let as ring-fenced holdings, albeit ones that could be easily divided.

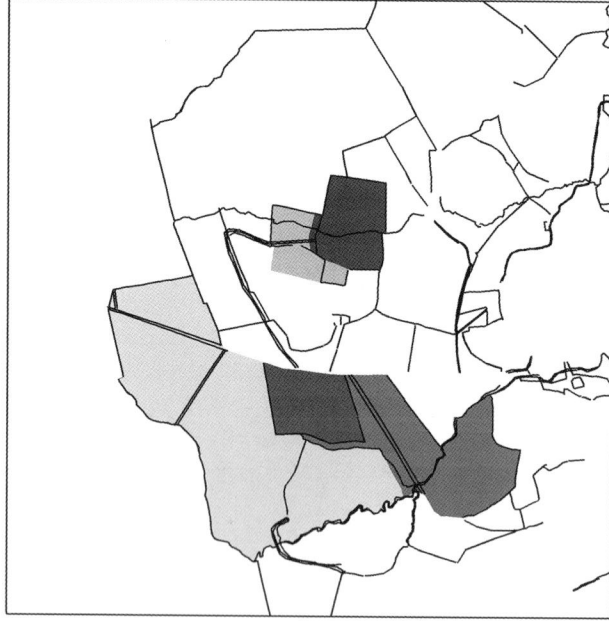

1731

1839

Dunshield
Flatt Allotment
Low Carrick
Middle Riding
South Riding

Fenwick Hedley's Farm
Joseph Patterson's Farm

N

km
0   0.5   1

Figure 3.3 Lands which were joined together between the enclosure and 1839. This eventually resulted in their going down to pasture. Based on the Elsdon Common enclosure award (NRO QRD3) and the tithe plan (NRO DT164M).

known to have been a ring-fenced farm in 1793, when a plan depicts it as such.[30] It is less clear whether the other two were ring-fenced. They are described as such in surveys of 1808, but this is only after both had been in hand.[31] This may well have led to major changes to their boundaries when they were let again after 1807. On balance, however, it is more likely that they were ring-fenced when they were named in 1772.

It is difficult to draw any firm conclusions from such evidence. However, until the late eighteenth century Howick certainly did not have standard ring-fenced farms. It is possible that the tenants always took the fields next to the rest of their land, thus creating ring-fenced farms in practice. Certainly, where their locations are known, fields from one lease tend to be in one area (Figure 3.2). This would have left the creation of ring-fenced farms up to the tenant. The landlord could easily have created a system in which ring-fenced farms were ensured by reorganising the estate. Unfortunately, with so little documentation in the crucial period it is not possible to determine whether the end of this system was the result of landlord or tenant action.

Thus far we have seen that tenants were clearly important in creating ring-fenced farms, perhaps because they had the most to gain from increased efficiency. In the examples discussed so far, however, landlords still played a role, as their permission was always required to change boundaries and they were in control of who received leases of their property. There are, nevertheless, cases in which the role of landlords is clearly less important.

Land under different tenures

In a few cases smallholders consolidated land of two different tenures by taking leasehold property adjoining their freehold farms. This happened at Milfield, as the earl of Tankerville, who received a very small allotment as lord of the manor at the 1789 enclosure of the common, leased this to the tenants of Francis Blake, who had a complete farm in Milfield.[32] In this case the tenants were entirely responsible for the consolidation as the lands involved were under different ownerships. Similarly, at Elsdon many tenants or smallholders consolidated land (Figure 3.3). For instance, the Flatt Fell, which was a particularly small allotment of the 1731 enclosure, was usually let to the tenant of the neighbouring Dunshield and Low Carrick, creating a more compact pattern of occupation. Thomas Thornton and his brother Robert Thornton provide a further example, as they united leasehold land with their freehold at Pearson's House in the south of the township. In all these cases smallholders were fully responsible for consolidation, as no landlord was involved.

30. DUSC GRE/X/P279.
31. DUSC GRE/X/P81.
32. NRO DT322S.

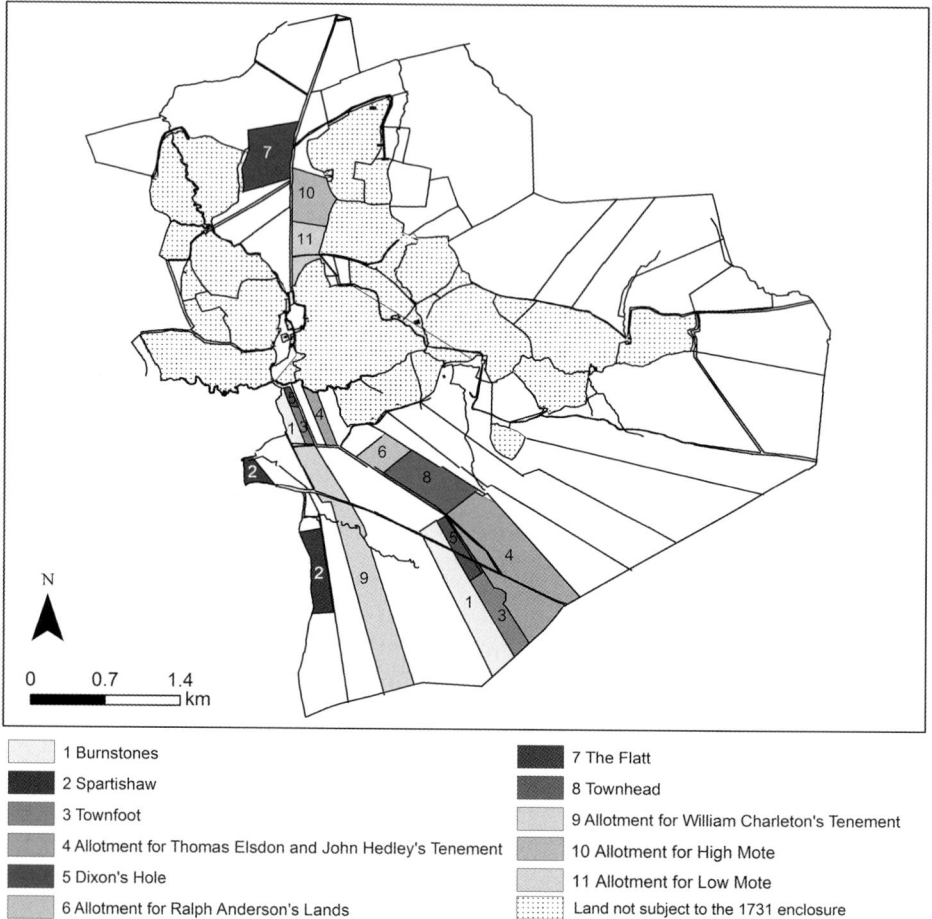

Figure 3.4 Allotments that were separated from their ancient lands in the 1731 enclosure of Elsdon, based on the Elsdon Common enclosure award (NRO QRD3). The allotment for High Mote could have been attached to its ancient lands by combining it with the allotment for Low Mote, to the south, but the opportunity was missed because of the complexity of its tenurial situation.

The influence of things

As with enclosure, the material environment in which consolidation occurred was as important as the people. This is most clear when material things formed barriers to consolidation. At Elsdon enclosure failed to create ring-fenced holdings because of the pre-existing pattern of holdings. It was unusual for parliamentary enclosures to create fragmented holdings, but in the case of Elsdon there was insufficient room around the ancient land for all 77 allotments to be placed next to the holdings to which they were allotted (Figure 3.4). The enclosure commissioners seem to have preferred to place a small part of the allotment near the holding and make the rest of the award further out on the common. For instance, a small block of land near the village was split into several small allotments for farms called Dixon's Hole, Townfoot and Burnstones, for which larger allotments were made further south. The case of Burnstones was further complicated by the fact that the majority of the ancient land of this holding was still unenclosed, meaning that there was no clear ancient holding for an allotment to be placed with. Difficulties of space could be overcome in some cases, particularly when a freeholder owned more than one farm. In such instances the allotment could be made for the area of all the farms of one person and then divided into the most convenient size for the space available at each. A clear example is the award for Shittleheugh, part of which was joined to the allotment for Killhouse, on the other side of the township.[33] The same was done with Edward Laing's allotments for Hillflex Rigg, Walls and Coxon's Field, and for the allotments made to unnamed owners at South Riding and North Bower Shields, and Landshot and Hudspeth East Field.[34] Finally, the fact that two of Charles Francis Howard's properties were treated in this way while one was not shows that it was not done in all such cases.[35] All of this means that farm consolidation events occurred in a variety of different ways as a result of particular combinations of freeholders, commissioners, the history of landholding and the meetings and discussion which took place between act and award.

It appears that a similar opportunity was missed at High Mote and Low Mote Farms in Elsdon because of the complexity of the title by which they were held. An agreement of 1729 devised the Low Mote to Elizabeth Hall and her second husband Matthew Hall for life. After this it was to go to Elizabeth's daughter by her first marriage, Catherine, and Catherine's husband Jeremiah Bayles. This altered the result of the will of Elizabeth's first husband, Robert Elsdon, who must have left it to her while she remained his widow.[36] It is likely that Matthew Hall owned Low Mote, as it was certainly the property of his son Alexander,[37] and other occupiers were often Halls.[38] It is possible that this meant that no one had the authority to direct the tenements to be joined together. Nonetheless, the situation was taken into account in the positioning of the tenements as the allotment for Low Mote was put next to that for High Mote. As we have seen with enclosure in the previous chapter, chance events and personal situations could be important forces in landscape change.

Thus, as with enclosure itself, a large number of forces, some of them very local or personal, influenced farm consolidation. Perhaps the most important

33. NRO QRD3.
34. NRO QRD3.
35. NRO QRD3.
36. NRO ZBS/26/2.
37. NRO ZBS/26/2.
38. *Elsdon Parish Register*, pp. 114, 141, 143, 164, 168, 171, 217, 221, 235.

point of this chapter is that tenants were tremendously important, playing a major role in nearly every case discussed here. Bigge's Quarter and Learmouth are especially clear examples, and even at Howick, where Edward Grey, the landlord, was important, tenants seem to have played a role, at least initially, in ensuring that Edward Grey's consolidated freehold was occupied as ring-fenced holdings. The efforts of tenants to create ring-fenced farms should not perhaps be surprising, as they worked the land and so stood to gain most through increased efficiency and convenience. The landlord's benefits are less clear. They profited from the success of their tenant's operations because the tenants were less likely to fall into arrears if their farms were easier to work. Convenient modern farms were also able to attract tenants more easily. Finally, landowners would have enjoyed the less tangible benefits of participating in a fashionable and virtuous activity. The role of landlords has been shown by other studies, but none have shown tenants to be as important as observed here.[39]

Discussion of the relative importance of landlords and tenants should not distract us from the other factors at work. As with enclosure, chance events such as the decline of the Herring family, the failure of Thomas Pinkney's farm or the complex legal situation of Low and High Mote at Elsdon were as important in determining exactly when and how consolidation occurred locally. Material objects are also important, although we have seen fewer examples of this than in our discussion of enclosure. The farms themselves were important in the parliamentary enclosure of Elsdon, as their large number and distribution added complications to the commissioners' task.

Thus, it has been shown here that the local reality of farm consolidation, like that of enclosure, was the result of the assemblage of many different and often unexpected people and things. This idea may also be explored in relation to another process which is often intimately linked to enclosure: the conversion of land between arable and pasture.

---

39. Moore-Colyer, 'Land and people'.

4

Rearranging the landscape

Changes to patterns of land use, such as the expansion of the arable area in the early nineteenth century, have often been unproblematically attributed to enclosure, but will be shown below to have only an indirect connection to it.[1] In Northumberland areas of permanent pasture and arable existed in both the pre- and post-enclosure periods, but the locations of these resources changed throughout the post-medieval period. It will be seen that a fairly clear pattern in the pre-enclosure landscape broke down as improvement progressed. The pattern was, however, never completely eradicated. Thus the incremental and contingent nature of the changes in land-use patterns are very similar to those associated with farm consolidation.

Changes in land use are reasonably well understood on a national scale, to the extent that we may relate a narrative for the post-medieval period. At the beginning of the post-medieval period (1550–1650) arable land was being converted to pasture.[2] At the same time convertible husbandry within unenclosed field systems became more significant. In this system land is put down to grass for several years then ploughed up for arable before being put down to grass again.[3] Such improvements may not have had significant productivity implications, but would certainly have altered the landscape.[4]

By the period 1660–1760 farming was becoming more mixed, and so, while much pasture was ploughed up, clay lands often went down to grass and parliamentary enclosure seems to have been used to create pasture.[5] When the Napoleonic Wars began, rising grain prices led to the creation of arable from pasture, which became an important aspect of parliamentary enclosure during

---

1. Yelling, Common field and enclosure, pp. 49–50, Beresford, Lost villages, pp. 11–17.
2. Yelling, Common field and enclosure, pp. 49–50.
3. Kerridge, The agricultural revolution.
4. Overton, Agricultural revolution in England.
5. A.H. John, 'The course of agricultural change 1660–1760', in L.S. Pressnell (ed.), Studies in the industrial revolution: presented to T.S. Ashton (London, 1960), pp. 145–9; Turner, English parliamentary enclosure, pp. 135–51.

this period.[6] After the Napoleonic Wars ended grain prices fell and consequently much of this new pasture went down to grass again.

During the eighteenth and nineteenth centuries regional patterns in land-use change begin to become discernable. For instance, it is well known that lowland heaths tended to become arable; that turnip rotations were adopted on limestone and chalk downs in the late eighteenth and early nineteenth centuries; and that much heavy clay land was put down to pasture after the Napoleonic Wars.[7] During this period technology, especially the use of lime and marl, was also important in the conversion of land from one use to another. For example, lime was used to improve Scottish wastes and outfields for arable cultivation,[8] while marl was important for the reclamation of acid heaths in East Anglia.[9] As a result it appears that enclosure was neither a necessary nor a sufficient condition for land-use change, although it is implicated in many cases.

Land conversion is an important part of post-medieval landscape dynamics and the agricultural revolution. Nonetheless, while it is well understood on regional and national levels, it has rarely been studied on a local scale. This chapter will attempt to show how local patterns of land use were altered during the post-medieval period. It will also determine whether these changes were permanent or, as other authors have suggested, whether the land often reverted from arable back to common waste. Finally, because several factors in addition to enclosure have been implicated, it will explore the extent to which land-use change was a product of enclosure.

Pre-enclosure patterns of land use

In order to understand the changes which took place in our townships during the agricultural revolution it is necessary to describe the pre-enclosure land-use patterns of Northumberland. In the county as a whole there were major differences between the coastal plains and interior vales, and the western uplands, the former being mostly arable and the latter mainly pastoral.[10] The lowlands show evidence of two- and three-field systems, but with some common waste at the margins. The uplands had much smaller areas of arable, sometimes with only one field, and extensive wastes that were exploited from shielings.[11] Both areas show evidence

6.   Turner, English parliamentary enclosure, pp. 135–51.
7.   H.C. Prince, 'The changing rural landscape', in G.E. Mingay (ed.), The agrarian history of England and Wales, Vol. VI (Cambridge, 1989), pp. 48–51.
8.   J.G. Harrison, 'East Flanders Moss, Perthshire: a documentary study', Landscape History, 30 (2008), pp. 5–19; R.A. Dodgshon, 'Land improvement in Scottish farming marl and lime in Roxburghshire and Berwickshire in the eighteenth century', Agricultural History Review, 26 (1978), pp. 1–14.
9.   Williamson, Transformation, pp. 67–70.
10. Butlin, 'Field systems'.
11. Butlin, 'Field systems'.

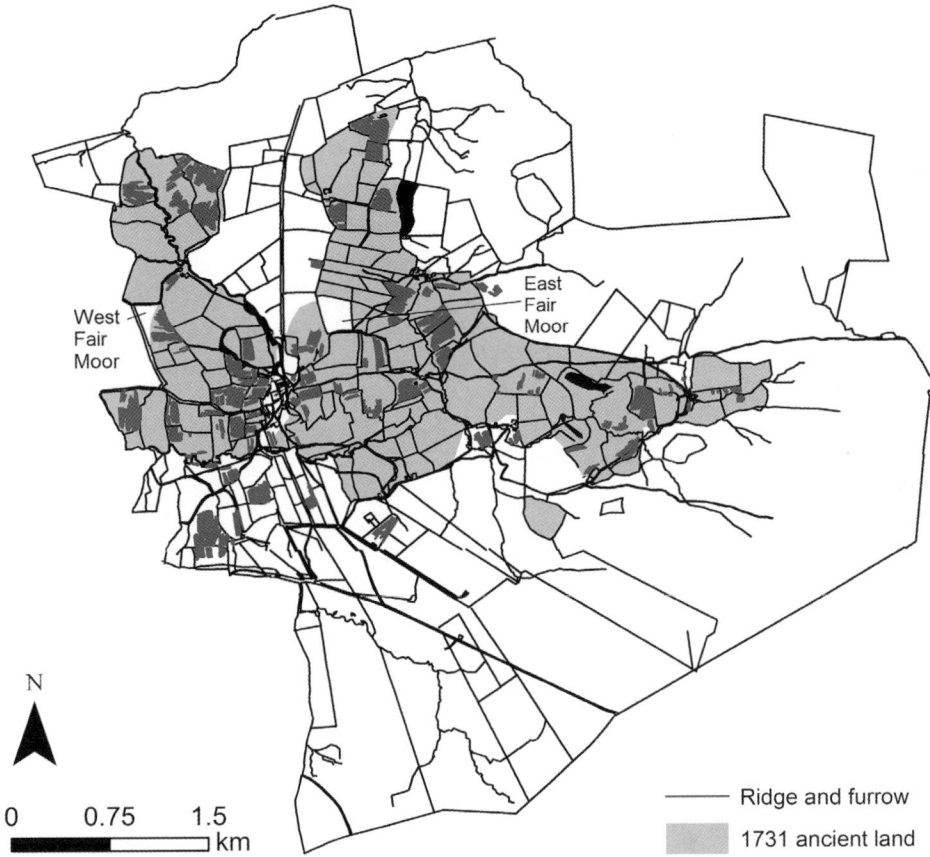

Figure 4.1 The distribution of ridge and furrow at Elsdon. It is largely confined to the ancient land, suggesting that this represents an arable core surrounded by the common, which was enclosed in 1731. Areas of the common must have been cultivated on occasion, however, as some ridge and furrow occurs outside the ancient land. The area of ancient land is taken from the Elsdon Common enclosure plan (NRO QRD3); the ridge and furrow is taken from aerial photographs held in the National Monuments Record and the Northumberland Historic Environment Record. For a full list of aerial photographs consulted see R.P. O'Donnell, 'Landscape agency and enclosure: transformations in the rural landscape of north-east England', PhD thesis (University of Durham, 2014).

Figure 4.2 Photograph showing that the difference between the arable core and common at Elsdon is clear even today, as the better-quality and more improved land of the arable core has a different flora to the former common and thus appears more green.

for the reclamation of waste, sometimes to create entire fields, and the occasional abandonment of arable at the margins of the cultivated area. Early maps and reconstructions of ancient field patterns appear to show a similar pattern of pre-enclosure land use, with commons at the edge and arable around the settlement.[12]

This pattern was certainly present in our townships. It is clearest at Elsdon, in the uplands, where the pattern of arable core and pastoral periphery can be seen on the 1731 enclosure plan (Figure 4.1). Here enclosure was of the common, so the ancient land represents, at least in part, the former arable core. This arable core occupied the floor of a valley in which the village also sat, while the common was located on both valley sides (Figure 4.2). Parts of this had gone down to grass by the time of the enclosure,[13] but there is evidence in the form of ridge and furrow (Figure 4.1), and the fact that some of the land was still held as unenclosed open-field strips, to show that most had been open-field arable.[14] There are only two

12. Butlin, 'Field systems'.
13. NRO ZBS/25/1, NRO ZHE/14/13, NRO 1356/14/1, NRO ZHE/14/31864, NRO ZBS/26/1, NRO ZHE/14/13.
14. NRO ZBS/25/1.

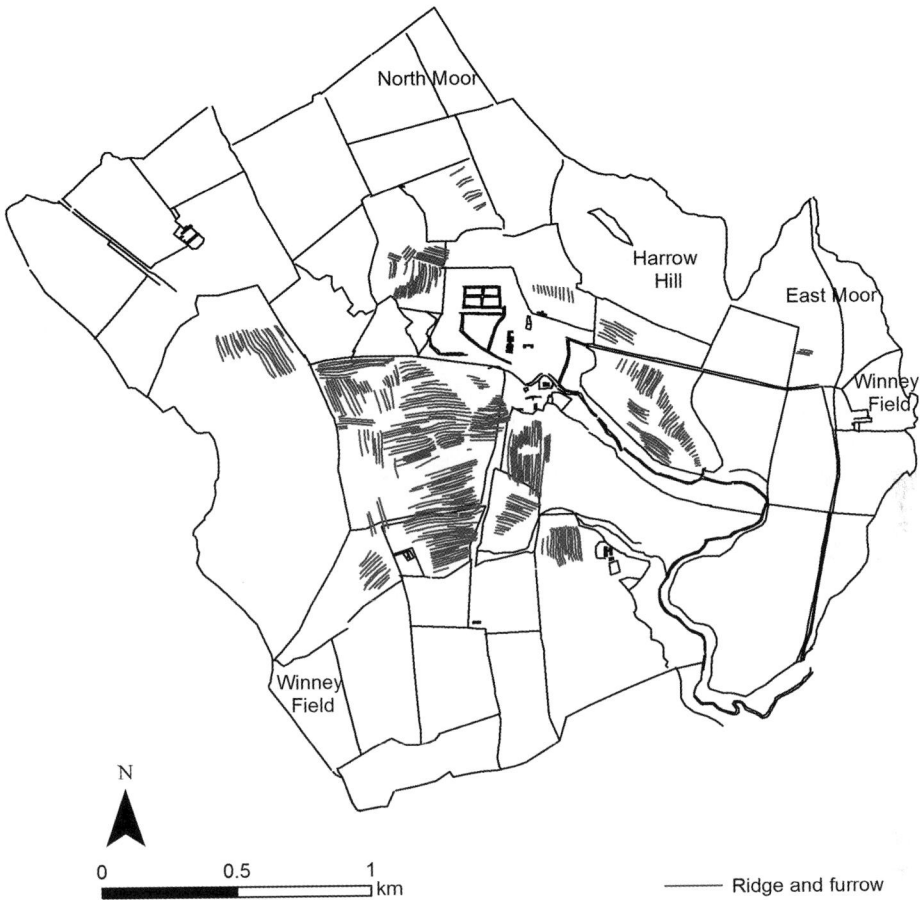

Figure 4.3 The distribution of ridge and furrow at Howick. As at Elsdon, this is concentrated in the centre of the township. The field-name elements 'moor' and 'winney' indicate patches of common at the edge of the township. The ridge and furrow is taken from photographs held in the Northumberland Historic Environment Record and the National Monuments Record.

exceptions to the pattern of arable core and pastoral periphery. The first was a small area of common within the ancient fields called West Fair Moor (Figure 4.1), but this was close to the edge of the ancient land. The second was a close on the common called Whitlees Sike. It is possible that this may have been arable, although it does not contain any ridge and furrow today.

At Howick and Longhorsley, on the coast and in the interior respectively, the pattern of arable core and pastoral periphery was less obvious but still present. At Howick there are two areas which may have been commons. The first is a group of fields called North Moor, East Moor and Harrow Hill (Figure 4.3). This possible common probably extended into Craster, where the field boundary forms suggest that it was enclosed piecemeal, although some ridge and furrow nearby suggests that it was of limited size (Figure 4.3). The element 'Moor' in the field names suggests poor-quality land that was likely to have been used as a common. Indeed, in Northumberland dialect 'Moor' can have the more specific meaning of 'common'.[15] More conclusive evidence for the use of this area as a common comes from the 1607 enclosure award. This instructed Edward Grey to compensate Mr Edmond Roddam for a beast gate on North Moor.[16] Another probable common was mentioned in a lease of The Heugh dated 1659, which gave the tenants access across Whinny Common. No Whinny Common is marked on any map of Howick, but there were two Whinny Fields on a plan of 1759: one near Sea Houses Farm and the other on the south-western township boundary, near Longhoughton. The second is more likely to be the Whinny Common mentioned in the 1659 deed as the clause in question appears to deal with access to Longhoughton, among other places. Unfortunately the document is damaged at this section so it is unclear if the route across Whinny Common was meant to allow access to Longhoughton or to another place. Nonetheless, this identification of the 1659 common is still more likely because the Whinny Field near Sea Houses would not allow access to anywhere other than the coast and Sea Houses Farm. The rest of the township appears to have been in arable cultivation immediately before enclosure, as there is ridge and furrow across most of it (Figure 4.3), and arable cultivation in the northern part of the township was mentioned in the 1607 enclosure award.[17] It is likely that the strong concentration of ridge and furrow near the village owes more to preservation bias than to the actual distribution of open-field arable, as this land was under grass for most of the post-medieval period. However, it does appear there was an open-field arable core with peripheral commons at Howick.

Longhorsley was very similar, although the evidence for peripheral commons is slighter than at Howick (Figure 4.4). In Bigge's Quarter Low Moor, West

15. J.T. Brockett, *A glossary of north country words in use, with their etymology and affinity to other languages and occasional notices of local customs and popular superstitions* (Newcastle-Upon-Tyne, 1829), p. 206.
16. DUSC GRE/X/P112.
17. DUSC GRE/X/P112.

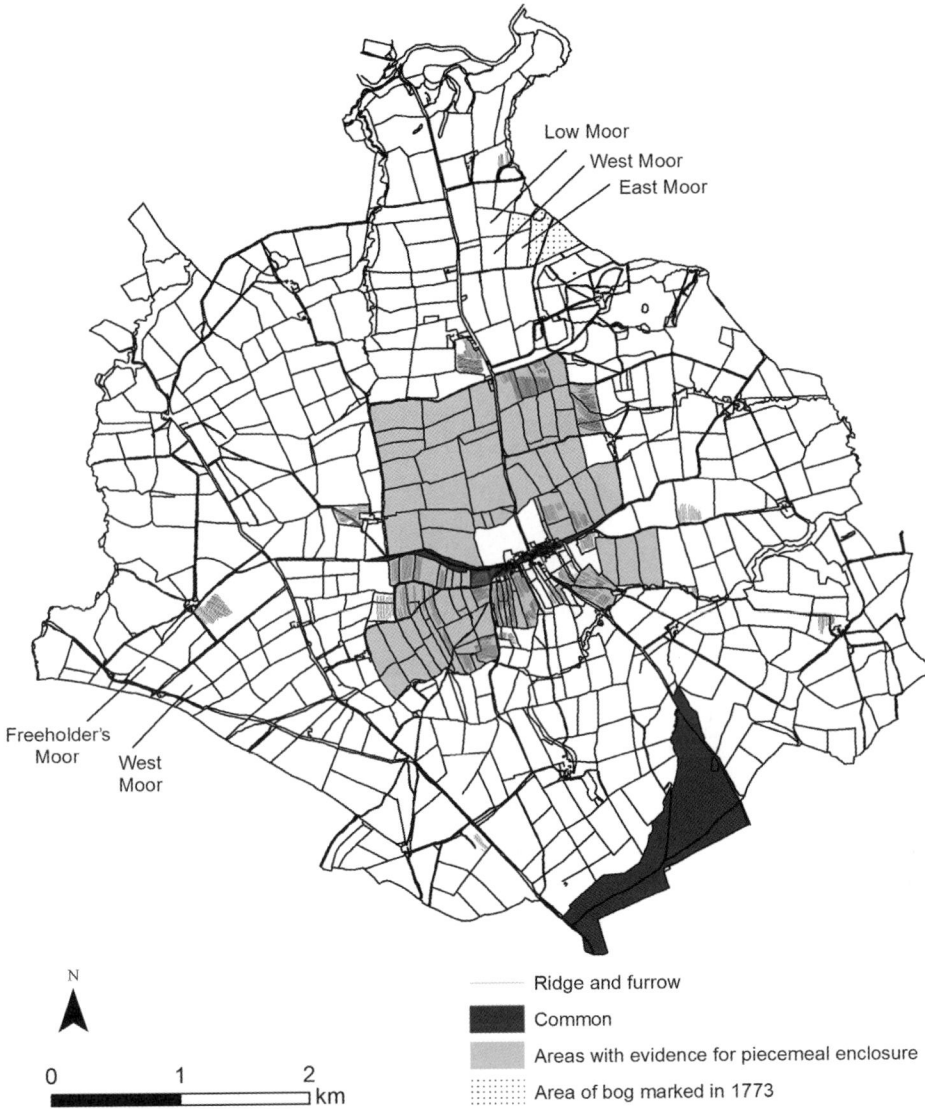

Low Moor
West Moor
East Moor

Freeholder's
Moor   West
          Moor

N

0   1   2
                    km

Ridge and furrow

Common

Areas with evidence for piecemeal enclosure

Area of bog marked in 1773

Figure 4.4 The distribution of ridge and furrow at Longhorsley. As at Elsdon and Howick, both the ridge and furrow and evidence for piecemeal enclosure are concentrated at the centre of the township, while the surviving common and some field names indicative of former common cluster at the edges. The ridge and furrow is taken from photographs held in the Northumberland Historic Environment Record and the National Monuments Record.

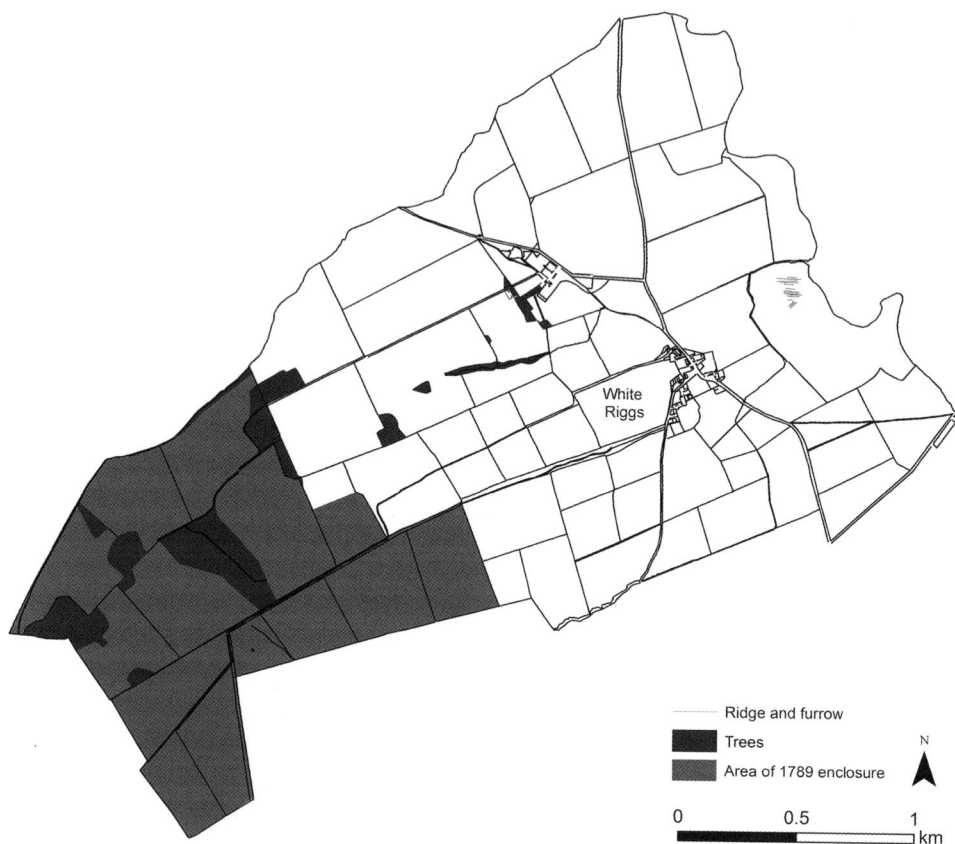

Figure 4.5 Milfield has less evidence for arable agriculture, although the 1789 enclosure of the common dealt solely with land in the west, while all evidence for arable agriculture is in the east. The fact that the two areas were enclosed separately also suggests that they had different uses.

Moor and East Moor fields are close together. Their names suggest poor-quality land, and they are depicted as boggy on a 1773 plan.[18] There is another area of 'moor' names at the western edge of Freeholder's Quarter, where there is a Freeholder's Moor and a West Moor.[19] Finally, an area of common in the south was preserved by the 1664 enclosure award.[20] Most of the evidence for open-field arable occurs near the village and appears to form an arable core. This consists of ridge and furrow and field boundaries suggesting piecemeal enclosure. Neither

18. CAS DHN/C/190/97.
19. NRO DT192M.
20. NRO 358/21/10.

of these types of evidence is likely to show the entire open-field area, as ridge and furrow survives only where there has been little later ploughing. Similarly, the distribution of piecemeal enclosure is unlikely to have been random within the open fields. However, as there is little evidence for commons near the village and abundant evidence for arable in this area there was probably an arable core and a pastoral periphery.

Milfield, which is in the north of the county, also had an arable core near the village and a common further out, although in this case the common was to one side of the arable, not surrounding it. In 1789 an area called Milfield or Lanton Common, which comprised roughly half the township, was enclosed (Figure 4.5). Consequently, it is certain that this area was common grazing in 1789.[21] The fact that the township was enclosed in two parts suggests, in itself, that there were different land uses in the two areas, implying that the land enclosed before 1789 had been arable. Further evidence for this is the higher quality of the ancient land,[22] the presence of ridge and furrow (Figure 4.5) and the field name elements 'Rig' and 'Ridges', which occur in the early enclosed land and probably refer to the ridge and furrow (Figure 4.5). As at Elsdon (Figure 4.2), the two land uses occupied different topographies, the arable being low-lying and the common on a hill. The common also occupied visibly poorer-quality land than did the arable, as it supported acid-loving species such as gorse (Ulex europaeus). It appears, then, that Milfield followed the familiar pattern of arable core and pastoral periphery.

Learmouth, also in the north of the county, has very little evidence for pre-enclosure land use. A 1756 lease says that one-fifth of the 'infield' should be summer fallowed, suggesting that this was in open-field strips, as it also required that no baulks be left between the ridges.[23] It also imposed a penalty for ploughing the 'outfield'. In Northumberland the terms infield and outfield probably refer to an area of intensive arable and an area of less intensively cultivated waste respectively; this may imply that a similar pattern to the other townships existed at Learmouth.[24] A plan of Learmouth made in 1793 supports this interpretation, as it marks Windy, East, Burn and Clover Fields near the village, which may form an arable core. It also shows large areas of bog containing 'night folds' in the south of the township, which may represent a common.[25] Unfortunately, without better information it is not possible to draw firm conclusions about the distribution of arable and pasture at Learmouth.

21. NRO QRD6.
22. Agricultural Land Classification <http://magic.defra.gov.uk/datadoc/results.asp?searchstring=l and+classification&search=S&x=0&y=0>, accessed 24 October 2012.
23. DUSC GRE/X/P75.
24. Butlin, 'Field systems', pp. 63–7.
25. DUSC GRE/X/P276.

This discussion suggests that, immediately before enclosure, many Northumberland townships consisted of an arable core near their settlement and common grazing further out. The proportion of arable to pasture varied geographically. The coastal and interior townships of Howick and Learmouth consist mostly of arable with small pockets of common at their edges, while commons in the uplands and the northern valleys at Elsdon, Learmouth and Milfield were much more extensive. However, pieces of arable were periodically put down to grass and pieces of the waste were occasionally cultivated.[26] Thus, the boundary between arable and pasture was not firmly fixed but changed over time. This may be observed in our townships. At Elsdon parts of the common seem to have been taken into arable cultivation. Parts of the ancient land marked on the 1731 enclosure plan seem to be former common, as there is no evidence for piecemeal enclosure in their field boundaries. These were, therefore, pieces of common that had been ploughed up. At Milfield there is also evidence that arable had encroached on the common, as legal opinions written in 1782 addressed the legality of some encroachments.[27] Similar, assarts were made on the common at Longhorsley, where the field names High Moor, North Moor and Low Moor, on the eastern edge of the common, may imply that pieces had been enclosed (Figure 4.4). There was probably also some encroachment from the north, as a legal case of 1870 records that Thomas Horsley had enclosed part of the common following the 1664 enclosure agreement.[28] It could be argued that this was enclosure, and thus a separate process from the periodic ploughing of pieces of common pasture which were then allowed to revert to waste, as Butlin suggests.[29] We have already seen the use of the terms 'infield' and 'outfield' at Learmouth, which may indicate such a practice. More convincing evidence for this practice also exists; as at Elsdon, there is pre-enclosure ridge and furrow on areas which were common in 1731 (Figure 4.1), although all of these are quite close to the ancient land. It appears to have been quite normal for pieces of waste to be cultivated, both in common and as closes. It was probably also usual for there to be some pasture or meadow closes near to the village, which further blurs the line between the arable core and pastoral periphery. There is evidence for this at Howick, as Edward Grey purchased some closes of meadow in 1581. These were probably close to the village, as they were sold with a tower.[30] Similarly, at Milfield the name Old Lea,

26. Butlin, 'Field systems', p. 109.
27. NRO 1356/M.5.
28. NRO 358/21/8. This case surrounded the right to the soil of Longhorsley common, which may have lain in two different manors. The issue arose because the 1664 enclosure award which divided Longhorsley manor did not define the southern boundary of Sir Horsley's portion. The making of assarts upon the common unopposed may be interpreted as evidence of his right to the soil.
29. Butlin, 'Field systems', p. 109.
30. DUSC GRE/X/P43.

next to the village, may recall a pasture close. Finally, the case of East Fair Moor at Elsdon, described above, is a further example of pasture within the arable area, though this time held in common.

To recap, there appears to have been a broad pattern of arable core and pastoral periphery in most Northumberland townships shortly before enclosure. The proportion of arable was higher on the coast and interior vales than in the uplands. There is evidence that the margins of these types of land use could be converted from one to another, both through small-scale enclosure and for common cultivation. There is also evidence for pockets of permanent pasture within the arable core of some of our townships. This broad pattern of arable core and pastoral periphery appears to break down further during the post-medieval period, though in a very drawn-out process.

Changing patterns of land use

In some cases large areas of former arable were put down to grass during the eighteenth and nineteenth centuries. This is clearest at Howick, where The Heugh and The Flatt, which contain ridge and furrow and are next to the village site, became a pasture used by the tenants of Pasture House and South Side Farms.[31] This is first documented in 1808, but may have originated earlier. Similarly, at Longhorsley, closes created by piecemeal enclosure appear to have been in use as pasture closes by the nineteenth century, as they were occupied individually and would have been too small to constitute individual arable farms.[32] These pastures may have been old, as pasture closes were allotted to Sir Thomas Horsley in 1664.[33] However, enclosure was not always necessary for the conversion of arable to pasture: at Elsdon, much unenclosed ancient land had been put down to grass by the nineteenth century. An 1809 lease of open-field property called the Batt, Townhead, Dunsdale and St Mary's Well shows that all but St Mary's Well were under grass, although a 1797 lease shows that the Batt had been in tillage only 12 years previously.[34] It is possible that this evidence may indicate ley farming, in which strips were put down to grass for a number of years before being cultivated again; however, this is uncertain as there is little evidence for the cultivation of these strips again during the nineteenth century. A valuation of unenclosed ridges

---

31. DUSC GRE/X/P81.
32. NRO DT43M, NRO DT391M.
33. NRO 358/21/10.
34. NRO ZBS/25/1, NRO ZHE/14/31864, NRO ZBS/26/1. It is possible that the duke was considering selling the land as part of a reorganisation of his holdings at Elsdon, as the surveyor remarked that 'Both these plots of ground would I doubt not be eagerly sought by some of the small freeholders living in or near the village – To the Ducal estate they are of small pecuniary value.'

belonging to the duke of Northumberland shows that they were also in grass.[35] Some enclosed land was also down to grass. A valuation of The Flatt and Mote Hills, which were enclosed parts of the ancient land, described them both as under grass in 1852, apart from two fields of The Flatt.[36] Some 1849 sale particulars describe Knightside and Spartishaw as 'nearly all in grass' and William Orde's farm at Hudspeth as 'chiefly in grass'.[37] Clearly parts of Elsdon's arable core had been put down to grass by the nineteenth century without the need for enclosure.

Evidence for the cultivation of waste is more problematic. At Longhorsley, Howick and Elsdon there are extensive areas of post-enclosure ridge and furrow which is mostly narrower and straighter than open-field ridge and furrow, and never has the typical reversed S-shape of the latter. Similar ridge and furrow has been excavated in southern Scotland, where it was produced between 1836 and 1869 for the improvement of pasture. This is supported by field observations at Elsdon, where some post-enclosure ridge and furrow has a markedly different flora from the surrounding heather moorland. This flora included species planted for improved swards such as perennial ryegrass (*Lolium perenne*) and clover (*Trifolium* spp.). Consequently, we cannot assume that post-enclosure ridge and furrow equates to arable cultivation, although the small size of the study area examined in Scotland does not allow us to reject the possibility that some, or even most, was indeed arable. On the other hand, it does represent the improvement of waste, which may be seen as a land-use change. In addition to this problem some eighteenth- and nineteenth-century cultivation certainly did not produce ridge and furrow, and some contemporaries even condemned the practice.[38] This means that ridge and furrow does not show the full extent of either post-enclosure arable husbandry or improved pasture.

It does, however, show that particular places were cultivated or improved. Unfortunately, it is too limited at Milfield and Learmouth to allow any conclusions to be drawn, but it is extensive at Howick, Longhorsley and Elsdon. In all of these places post-enclosure cultivation or improvement extended to the edges of the townships and included former common. At Longhorsley the surviving common was not cultivated or improved because it was still legally protected, but ridge and furrow extended right up to it, and former common in Freeholder's Quarter was cultivated. In the south of Elsdon ridge and furrow is concentrated around

---

35. NRO ZHE/14/13. This survey, on the other hand, seems to have been intended to assess what improvements could be made to the Mote Hills and The Flatt, as it is presented in the form of a printed questionnaire which asks specifically for recommendations on the course of husbandry and the buildings. The only recommendation made by the surveyor was to put the two cultivated fields down to grass.
36. NRO ZHE/14/13.
37. NRO 1356/14/1.
38. S. Upex, 'A classification of ridge and furrow by an analysis of cross-profiles', *Landscape History*, 26 (2004), pp. 59–75.

farmhouses built on the former common, suggesting that it was part of a wider programme of improvement of former waste. These farmhouses were often built by wealthy investors, and so the conversion of land from waste to arable or improved pasture may have required wealth. The best example is Pearson's House, which was probably built by Thomas Pearson, who had bought the land with money made at his quarry in Walbottle.[39] The farm is surrounded by post-enclosure ridge and furrow that stops at its boundary, suggesting that the two are associated. This implies that enclosure alone did not cause land-use change. At Longhorsley, on the other hand, post-enclosure ridge and furrow is found in nearly all fields, suggesting that all farmers were able to utilise this practice. The better land quality at Longhorsley (Grades 3 and 4 in the five-point Agricultural Land Classification) may have made improvement more worthwhile than at Elsdon (Grades 4 and 5), where it was more restricted.[40] This may be supported by the evidence at Howick, which also has extensive post-enclosure ridge and furrow. Here almost all areas are covered except a large area of pasture in the middle of the township (Figure 4.3). Some of this ridge and furrow was certainly arable during the nineteenth century as documents record crops produced in these fields, though it is possible that some was improved pasture.

It appears that from enclosure onwards patterns of land use changed. Much of the former pattern of arable core and pastoral periphery was destroyed, producing landscapes with no obvious land-use pattern. This occurred through both the grassing down of parts of the arable and the ploughing up or improvement of pieces of common. Some of the forces behind this have been suggested. For example, the fact that the improvement of the common at Elsdon is associated with the newly constructed farmsteads of wealthy investors suggests that both enthusiasm and the availability of capital may have been important in facilitating change. On the other hand, the influence of things and ideas may be discerned by comparing Howick and Longhorsley with Elsdon. At both Howick and Longhorsley better-quality land encouraged much more extensive improvement and cultivation than at Elsdon. It has also been shown that enclosure was not a completely necessary prerequisite, as much of Elsdon's nineteenth-century open fields had been put down to grass without it. Enclosure may, however, have speeded the process.

The survival and re-emergence of pre-enclosure patterns

These changes to the old pattern of land use were never complete. In detail, elements of the pre-enclosure pattern of land use often survived enclosure or returned after it. At Howick, for instance, the common in the north of the

---

39. NRO ZBS/26/2.
40. Agricultural Land Classification <http://magic.defra.gov.uk/datadoc/metadata.asp?dataset=2>, accessed 15 August 2012.

township was still unimproved in 1759, approximately 150 years after its enclosure (Figure 4.3). In that year a map shows it as an unfenced boggy area. It may have been divided and improved shortly after this, as the boundaries which had divided East Moor before the making of the 1866 Ordnance Survey map were added to the 1759 plan in pencil. Parts of the area contain post-enclosure ridge and furrow and much of it was in arable cultivation by 1845, though part remained under grass.[41] If the improvement did occur shortly after 1759 it may have been carried out as part of the wider landscape changes which accompanied the rebuilding of the hall in 1782.[42] These changes included the relocation of the village onto the former moor in the same area as the boundaries.[43] These alterations were made at the instigation of Sir Henry Grey[44] and reflected the rise of the Greys, who had been created baronet a generation previously.[45]

At Longhorsley, a large part of the common was retained in the 1664 enclosure award and so continued in that form.[46] Another area of former common, called Cold Walls, which was enclosed (in the sense of having common rights abolished) at least as early as 1664, remained unimproved in 1773 when a map represented it as unfenced and boggy.[47] This appears to have been improved by 1866,[48] but it is unknown whether it was converted to arable. It was ploughed into ridges and drained with ceramic pipes, some of which have been recovered from it. The particularly imprecise dating of the event means that it is impossible to place it in a context. This was, however, a period which included the post-Napoleonic War boom and the mid-nineteenth-century period of favourable prices.

Finally, at Milfield the common was still being improved in 1815, 26 years after its enclosure. This is described in a lease of that year in which John Grey, the tenant of Milfield Hill Farm, was instructed to divide Burn Close into three pieces and

> divide one of the Fields called the Outfields (and which contains thirty seven acres) into two Inclosures of equal Quantity And also that he or they shall and will inclose with a substantial stone wall from that part of the said Premises called the

41. DUSC GRE/X/P270.
42. N. Pevsner and I.A. Richmond, *The buildings of England: Northumberland* (1957; 5th edn, London, 1987), p. 194.
43. DUSC GRE/X/P276.
44. Pevsner and Richmond, *Northumberland*, p. 194.
45. Bateson, *Northumberland*, p. 352.
46. NRO 358/21/10.
47. CAS C/190/97.
48. First edition Ordnance Survey map 1:10,560 1866 <http://digimap.edina.ac.uk/historicdownloader/downloader;jsessionid=5B687A18BE1F83F10AA3ED16E5A62A5C?execution=e1s1>, accessed 12 March 2012.

Figure 4.6 Gorse on the former Milfield Common shows that it is poor-quality land. The plantation in the background was an alternative use for land that was unsuitable for agriculture.

> Allotment adjoining the said Outfield a field or inclosure to contain not less than thirty five acres of Land.[49]

All this suggests that much of the common was rough grass at the time. The lease also required John Grey to plant trees at Ewe Hill, which was one of several beech and pine plantations made on the former common after enclosure (Figure 4.5).[50] This suggests that the common was on land of such poor quality that its owners, the Greys of Howick, thought it best to use it for game or timber. Indeed, it remains poor quality today, with large quantities of gorse (*Ulex europaeus*) indicating acid soils (Figure 4.6). The other two Milfield farms have no trees on their common allotments, suggesting that other owners did use the former common entirely as agricultural land. These changes to the landscape coincide with two important events in the history of the township. The first is the inheritance of the Howick estate, of which Milfield forms a part, by the second Earl Grey in 1808. He seems to have begun a programme of improvement which continued for several years, of

49. DUSC GRE/X/P79.
50. DUSC GRE/X/P79, First edition Ordnance Survey 1:10,560 1866 <http://digimap.edina.ac.uk/ historicdownloader/downloader;jsessionid=5B687A18BE1F83F10AA3ED16E5A62A5C?executio n=e1s1>, accessed 12 March 2012; NRO DT322S.

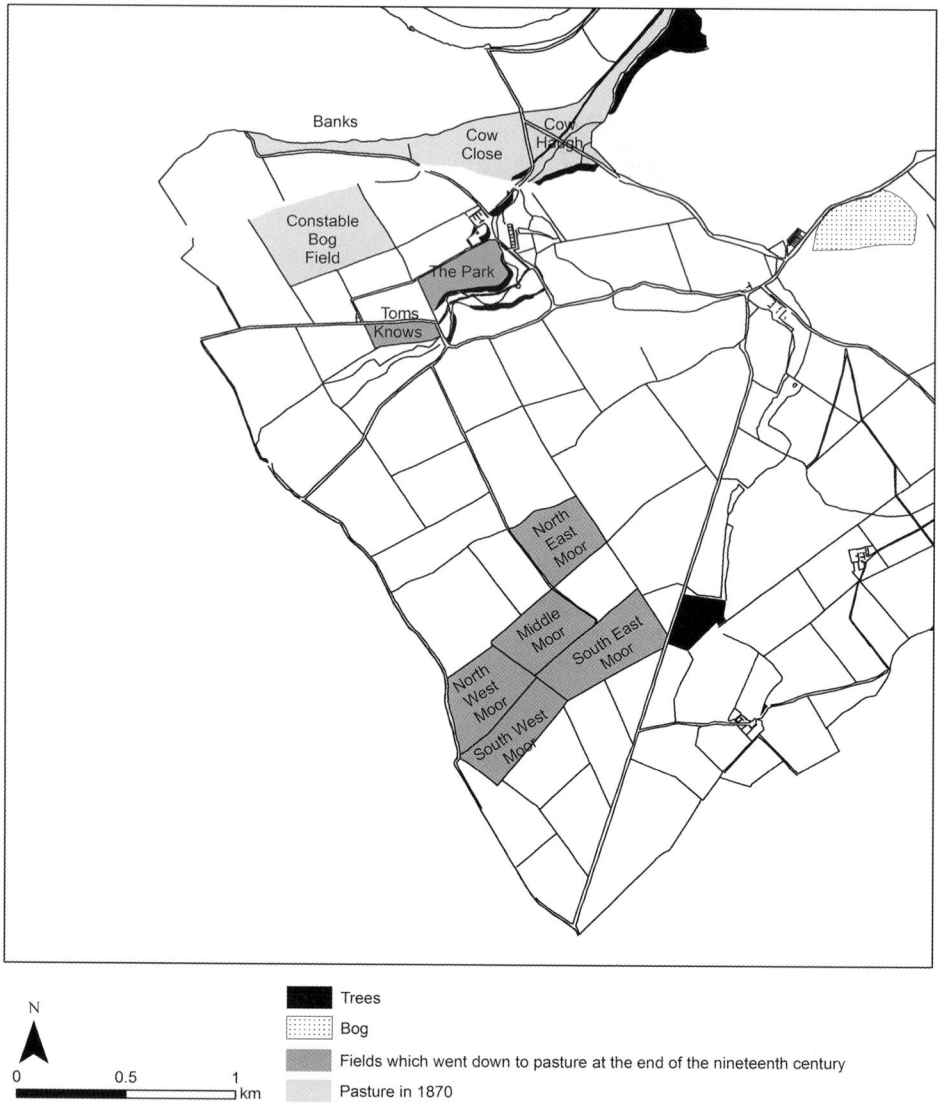

Figure 4.7 Fields which went down to pasture at Learmouth at the end of the nineteenth century. Many of these are on former common land in the south, showing that improvement did not entirely eradicate former patterns of land use. Land use data is taken from the Cultivation Returns (DUSC GRE/X/P271).

which the changes at Milfield may have been a part. Certainly, the plantations must be the work of the landowner, as the trees and game were his property according to the terms of the lease, and so were useless to the tenant. The other event was the coming of age of John Grey, who occupied Milfield Hill Farm. John had in practice been the tenant since his father's death in c.1803, but because of his minority the farm was held for him by trustees.[51] His majority in 1815 appears to have been the opportunity for improvement. These improvements may have been the initiative of the landlord, who requested them in the lease, or at John Grey's suggestion, who had them put in the lease to make the landlord's consent more secure. John Grey was known as an improver, so he probably would have at least taken an interest in these matters.[52]

As well as being partially retained, old land-use patterns could also re-emerge, as former wastes were the most likely places to go down to pasture in adverse economic conditions. At Learmouth several fields were put down to grass according to the 'cultivation returns', which are available for West Learmouth Farm in a nearly complete sequence from 1870 to 1890.[53] These show that the vast majority of fields were used for arable cultivation throughout the period, in stark contrast to the large areas of common waste shown in 1793.[54] Only Banks and Cow Close are never mentioned and were therefore in permanent pasture throughout the period. Some other fields were present on the cultivation returns but were always described as pasture, suggesting that they had gone down to grass shortly before 1870. These fields were mostly in the north, but one called North Haugh and Hare Knows is not marked on any plan (Figure 4.7).[55] Of the remaining fields, several went down to pasture during the late nineteenth century. The first were Toms Knows and The Park, which went down to grass between 1873 and 1887 and 1873 and 1886 respectively before being ploughed up again (Figure 4.7).[56] Toms Knows was almost certainly within the ancient cultivated area and so shows that the ancient pattern of land use did not entirely re-emerge in the late nineteenth century. From 1883 onwards several fields went down to grass in the south of the township (Figure 4.7).[57] Several of these contain the element 'Moor' in their

51. DUSC GRE/X/P35.

52. Butler, Memoir of John Grey.

53. DUSC GRE/X/P271. These documents were forms filled in by each of the tenants of the Howick estate and returned to the land agent so that the estate could monitor the rotations used. They consist of a printed list of the fields, next to which the tenant wrote the crop sown in each field in the current year. While these are available for East Learmouth they are less complete and the field names here are poorly understood, so the distribution of cultivation in the landscape cannot be assessed.

54. DUSC GRE/X/P276.

55. DUSC GRE/X/P271.

56. DUSC GRE/X/P271.

57. DUSC GRE/X/P271.

names, and it is thus tempting to link them with the ancient common waste. This seems to be confirmed by the presence of a night fold, indicating grazing, and bogs in this area on the 1793 plan.[58] It appears, then, that while parts of the ancient arable area at Learmouth were put down to pasture during the agricultural depression, the majority of the land put down to grass was former common. This means that the ancient land-use pattern had only been partly eradicated. It may be significant that the fields begin to go down to pasture in 1873, as this was the year after William Piper Lumsden became tenant.[59] He struggled to run the farm during the depression and was ultimately forced to leave. It may be this struggle to make a profit from the farm which led to the fields going down to pasture.

At Longhorsley there was another instance of improved arable reverting to rough grazing. At the southern end of Smallbourne Farm some fields are shown as fenced in 1777.[60] They were definitely cultivated or improved as they contain post-enclosure ridge and furrow which conforms to the 1777 field boundaries. By 1866 the boundaries were removed and the area had become boggy, and so was probably rough grazing.[61] The phenomenon is even clearer at Elsdon, where most of the former common returned to rough grazing after enclosure. Here the boundaries at the Flatt Fell created following the 1731 enclosure were removed, suggesting that the area had reverted to rough grazing. This had definitely been cultivated or improved earlier, as it contains ridge and furrow. Mid-nineteenth-century surveys describe the Flatt Fell as rough pasture in 1852 and 1868, suggesting that it had been allowed to revert to waste by that time.[62] It was let to the tenant of Dunshield and Low Carrick, which surrounds the Flatt Fell.[63] This allowed it to be joined onto Dunshield and Low Carrick in order to create a large expanse of rough grazing. Dunshield and Low Carrick, as the name suggests, was also an amalgamation of two farms. This amalgamation allowed the boundaries between their allotments to be taken down, probably indicating that they too had been made into rough pasture. Bainshaw Bog appears to have been subject to a similar process. This area was divided between the glebe of Alwinton and Lowick after its enclosure and a boundary made between the two by 1839.[64] By 1866 this boundary had been partly removed and it is likely that the Thornton family, who owned the neighbouring Pearson's House, were using it as waste. It was described as rough pasture in an 1864 lease, and the boundaries between it and Pearson's

58. DUSC GRE/X/P276.
59. DUSC GRE/X/P254.
60. NRO 1255/1.
61. First edition Ordnance Survey map 1:10,560 1866 <http://digimap.edina.ac.uk/historicdownloader/downloader;jsessionid=5B687A18BE1F83F10AA3ED16E5A62A5C?execution=e1s1>, accessed 12 March 1012.
62. NRO ZHE/14/13.
63. NRO ZHE/14/13.
64. NRO DT164M.

House had been allowed to go down.[65] Similarly, boundaries between allotments for properties at Landshot and East Nook went down between 1731 and 1866, creating a very large area of rough grazing. These farms were owned by the Ordes of Nunnikirk in 1839. Orde properties were also joined together to create a large open farm out of the enclosure allotments for Redshaw, Knightside and John's Croft between 1731 and 1839.[66] By 1866 this area was completely unfenced, and thus probably rough grazing. It had also been enlarged by the addition of the allotment for William Charlton's Croft.[67] The fact that both of these were owned by the Orde family in 1839 may suggest that one of the Ordes allowed all the farms to revert to waste, although the Ordes were not the owners in 1731 so this is not certain. All this suggests that large areas of the common were allowed to become rough pasture during the nineteenth century despite some having been improved, or even cultivated, shortly before. Unfortunately, the imprecise dating of these events at Elsdon and Longhorsley does not allow them to be put in context as successfully as have the events at the other three townships. The period in which they occur did, however, contain two agricultural depressions – one after the Napoleonic Wars and another in the late nineteenth century – which may have caused some of them.

To sum up, changes to patterns of land use after enclosure were rarely complete and could be reversed. Many former commons remained waste without common grazing rights long after enclosure, awaiting the right circumstances for their improvement. At Howick the improvement of the common appears to have been delayed until the rise of the Grey family. This triggered landscape changes including the relocation of the village onto the common (see Chapter 5), providing the opportunity to divide and improve other parts of it. At Longhorsley the improvement of Cold Walls may have been allowed by the period of relatively high agricultural produce prices in the mid-nineteenth century. The improvement of the part of Milfield Common in Milfield Hill Farm appears to have been left until two enthusiastic improvers, one the landowner and the other the tenant, arrived to take it on.

On the other hand, many pieces of former common which had been made into arable were allowed to go down to pasture. At Learmouth good dating evidence shows that much occurred in the 1880s and 1890s, during the agricultural depression. At Elsdon reversion to pasture seems to have occurred before the late nineteenth-century depression, and could have happened during the depression following the Napoleonic Wars. Here some of the reversion of arable to waste is associated with the Orde family, who may have been more active than others in

65. NRO ZHE/14/31864, NRO ZBS/26/1.
66. NRO QRD3, NRO DT164M.
67. First edition Ordnance Survey map 1:10,560 1866 <http://digimap.edina.ac.uk/ historicdownloader/downloader;jsessionid=5B687A18BE1F83F10AA3ED16E5A62A5C?executio n=e1s1>, accessed 12 March 1012.

allowing it to happen. The effects of the depression at Learmouth also appear to have been influenced by the reactions of particular individuals, since fields began to go down to grass when William Piper Lumsden succeeded his father. Finally, it is important to note that, at the same time, fields which had been arable before enclosure were also going down to pasture, so this was not a complete reversion to the pre-enclosure pattern of land use.

The developments at Learmouth are typical of the complexity of land-use change, in which each event is contingent on all elements involved. Nevertheless, we may draw some general conclusions. There was clearly a particular pattern of land use in Northumberland townships prior to enclosure, which comprised an arable core and a pastoral periphery. It differed regionally, with a higher proportion of arable in coastal and interior townships, reducing commons to small pockets at the township edges. Upland townships had much more extensive commons which surrounded the arable. The pattern was not completely rigid, as it seems to have been quite normal for pieces of arable to be allowed to go down to grass and parts of the common to be ploughed up when the need arose.

This pattern began to change in the post-medieval period, with more extensive areas of the common being taken into cultivation and large areas of the arable cores being allowed to go down to grass. The latter process appears to have begun before enclosure, as much of the unenclosed open-field land at Elsdon was under grass in the nineteenth century. Enclosure may have accelerated the process, as much land seems to have been improved for either pasture or arable soon after. Some areas, particularly those of former commons, however, remained unimproved long after enclosure, showing that the process did not depend on enclosure alone. There is some evidence that particular people were more involved than others in the process of improving former commons, as ridge and furrow at Elsdon appears to be associated with farmhouses built by wealthy investors. It is likely that the post-enclosure landscape was more organised than has been discussed here, as, for instance, it is occasionally suggested that enclosure allowed particular crops to be planted on the most appropriate land.[68] Unfortunately records are rarely detailed enough to map the cultivation of particular crops and so it has not been possible to assess this sort of information in our case studies. It is also important to realise that crops were rotated and thus nearly all arable fields were used to grow all types of crops, though, as we shall see below, different rotations were used on different areas of Learmouth towards the end of the nineteenth century.

The changes were not always permanent, as it appears quite normal for former common to revert to rough grazing. At Learmouth this occurred during a time of agricultural depression, suggesting that economic trends had a part to play. It is, however, important to note that former open-field arable also went down to pasture at this time: there was no complete return to the former pattern of land use.

68. Williamson, *Transformation*.

It has been possible to determine some of the factors involved in both the removal and partial reinstatement of the early pattern of land use. In some cases particular people are significant, such as William Lumsden, whose arrival seems to have triggered the conversion of fields from arable to pasture. Similarly, at Elsdon the Orde family owned several areas which were put down to grass during the nineteenth century. The availability of money also seems to have been significant, with much reversion to pasture occurring during the agricultural depression of the late nineteenth century. Thus, while William Lumsden made the decision to put fields down to grass where others may have kept them in tillage, it was a decision which had to be made only under particular circumstances. Finally, it must be remembered that the land itself played a part, as some commons were left unimproved after enclosure, and probably became common grazing in the first place, because they were of low quality and expensive to improve. This is why some of these areas were the first to revert to pasture during difficult times.

These processes are very complex and uneven. Despite the presence of many exceptions it is apparent that the pre-enclosure pattern of arable core and pastoral, or only occasionally cultivated, periphery was removed during the post-medieval period. Such complexity was not only a feature of processes intimately associated with enclosure, such as land-use change and farm consolidation, but also of processes which are more indirectly attributed to enclosure, including settlement dispersal, which will form the subject of the next chapter.

5

Dispersing settlement

In most historical literature the processes described in the two preceding chapters are so closely connected with enclosure as to be considered inseparable from it. Other types of post-medieval landscape change, however, are often portrayed as a consequence of enclosure rather than part of enclosure itself. One such change is settlement dispersal.

A combination of settlement creation and desertion typically caused dispersal during the post-medieval period.[1] In our townships both processes were governed by multiple factors, and as a result are as complex as the other processes we have examined so far. It is interesting that scholarly attention has usually focused on settlement desertion,[2] although some work has considered settlement dispersal as an aspect of this process.[3] However, the occurrence of settlement dispersal *without* village desertion has not been sufficiently investigated. The published literature deals with the phenomenon only when it is the result of the expansion of the arable area.[4] Consequently, a discussion of the full range of settlement dynamics is required. This is attempted below, and demonstrates that there are similarities in the settlement dynamics of townships in which village depopulation did occur and those where it did not. This examination will begin with village desertion, as it has attracted most attention in published work.

1. Williamson, *Transformation*, pp. 46–7; M. Beresford, 'A review of historical research', in M. Beresford and J.G. Hurst (eds), *Deserted medieval villages: studies* (London, 1971), pp. 3–75; S. Wrathmell, 'Deserted and shrunken villages in southern Northumberland from the twelfth to the twentieth centuries', PhD thesis (University of Wales, 1975).
2. Beresford, *Lost villages*; Beresford, 'Review of historical research'; Wrathmell, 'Deserted and shrunken villages'; Wrathmell, 'Village depopulation'; M.L. Parry, 'Secular climate change and marginal agriculture', *Transactions of the Institute of British Geographers*, 64 (1975), pp. 1–13.
3. Wrathmell, 'Deserted and shrunken villages'; Dixon, 'Deserted villages of Northumberland'.
4. Brown, 'Post-enclosure farmsteads'; J. Bettey, 'Downlands', in J. Thirsk (ed.), *Rural England: an illustrated history of the landscape* (Oxford, 2002), p. 44.

Village desertion

A small amount of settlement desertion occurred during the medieval period as a result of, for example, the creation of granges by Cistercian monks in Yorkshire.[5] Nationally, however, the main period of village desertion occurred during the period 1450–1520.[6] During this period desertion was caused by the engrossing of peasant holdings in order to create sheep pasture as wool prices remained high and grain prices fell. This is, however, a much less important phase in the history of village depopulation in Northumberland.[7] During the seventeenth and eighteenth centuries enclosure more widely ceased to be purely for sheep pasture and was used more for mixed farming, leading to reduced levels of village desertion on a national scale.[8] In Northumberland, however, desertion became more common during this period.[9] Large-scale landscape reorganisation involving agricultural improvement and enclosure often included the desertion of nucleated settlements in favour of dispersed farmsteads.[10] This has been observed in the archaeological survey of West Whelpington, where two farmsteads were built during the seventeenth century and before the desertion of the village in the eighteenth century.[11] Finally, eighteenth-century emparkment was also a cause of settlement desertion. This usually occurred in closed townships with resident landlords.[12] This type of depopulation has also been observed archaeologically during the Shapwick project, where only part of the village was depopulated in order to create a park. The process appears to have been completed rapidly and removed all traces of the settlement.[13]

Aspects of several of these processes, particularly seventeenth-century landscape reorganisation and improvement, can be observed at Howick and Learmouth.[14] At Howick depopulation was preceded by a long process of engrossment by Sir Edward Grey of Morpeth,[15] who was a cadet of an established

5.   Beresford, *Lost villages*, pp. 4–8; Beresford, 'Review of historical research', pp. 151–5.

6.   Beresford 'Review of historical research', p. 11.

7.   Beresford, *Lost villages*, pp. 150, 172–5; Wrathmell, 'Deserted and shrunken villages'; Dixon, 'Deserted villages of Northumberland'.

8.   Beresford, 'Review of historical research', p. 19.

9.   Wrathmell, 'Deserted and shrunken villages'; Dixon, 'Deserted villages of Northumberland'.

10. Wrathmell, 'Village depopulation'; Dixon, 'Deserted villages of Northumberland', pp. 245–58.

11. D.H. Evans, M.G. Jarrett and S. Wrathmell, 'The deserted village of West Whelpington, Northumberland: third report, part two', *Archaeologia Aeliana*, 16 (1988), pp. 155–9.

12. Beresford, *Lost villages*, pp. 139–41; T. Williamson, '"At pleasure's lordly call": the archaeology of emparked settlements', in C. Dyer and R.L.C. Jones (eds), *Deserted villages revisited* (Hatfield, 2010), pp. 162–81; Dixon, 'Deserted villages of Northumberland', pp. 247–9.

13. Gerrard, 'A rural landscape explored', p. 1001; C.M. Gerrard and M.A. Aston, *Interpreting the English village: landscape and community at Shapwick, Somerset* (Oxford, 2013).

14. Wrathmell, 'Deserted and shrunken villages'; Dixon, 'Deserved villages of Northumberland'.

15. DUSC GRE/X/P43.

Northumbrian family.[16] He may have exercised these connections in his initial purchase of a tower and three acres of meadow from his brothers Roger and Arthur Grey of Chillingham in 1593.[17] He then continued to buy out freeholders until 1607, when he made an enclosure agreement with John Craster. This effectively separated the lands owned by John Craster from the open fields,[18] but the open fields appear to have remained in operation in the rest of the township.[19] Further purchases up to 1623 allowed Grey to gain unity of possession of the remaining unenclosed lands.[20] A plan of 1759 shows a very regular, and thus apparently planned, arrangement of field boundaries, suggesting that Edward Grey or one of his successors had reorganised and enclosed the township.[21] As rentals and deeds from 1635 onwards mention the names of closes marked on the 1759 plan it is likely that the enclosure of the open fields occurred between 1623 and 1635.[22] Engrossment did not lead to the immediate abandonment of the village, which is depicted on the 1759 plan. It did, however, move the farms out of the village, which was an important precursor to depopulation at other Northumberland villages such as West Whelpington.[23] The 1759 plan shows five farmsteads in the surrounding fields. One of these is marked as the steward's house, and so may be identified as the home farm.[24] The remaining four probably correspond to the four farms listed in a 1756 rental.[25] The desertion of the village seems to have happened in 1782, during emparkment of the area to the south of the newly built hall.[26] The first evidence of the village having been deserted is a plan of 1791,[27] while a plan of Sea Houses Farm to the west of Howick Hall drawn in 1793 shows roads going to the site of the new model village.[28] Several field names in the area of the new village contain the word 'moor', suggesting that they lay on marginal land. The depopulation was almost certainly carried out for aesthetic reasons, as the village would have blocked views both towards and from the hall (Figure 5.1). The immediately pre-depopulation village depicted in mid-eighteenth-century plans appears to have been small, as was its successor, which contained 11 cottages in 1801.[29] The events leading to depopulation at Howick largely fit the

16. Bateson, *Northumberland*, p. 349.
17. DUSC GRE/X/P43.
18. DUSC GRE/X/P112.
19. DUSC GRE/X/P43.
20. DUSC GRE/X/P43.
21. DUSC GRE/X/P276.
22. DUSC GRE/X/P94, DUSC GRE/X/P43, DUSC GRE/X/P276.
23. Evans *et al.*, 'West Whelpington'.
24. DUSC GRE/X/P276.
25. DUSC GRE/X/P80.
26. Pevsner and Richmond, *Northumberland*, p. 194.
27. DUSC GRE/X/P276.
28. DUSC GRE/X/P279.
29. DUSC GRE/X/P181.

Figure 5.1 View towards Howick Hall across the deserted village site, which occupies the area of daffodils in the foreground. It is likely that the village was depopulated in order to create this view, which was further maintained through the creation of a ha-ha (not in shot) at the bottom of the slope between the house and the village site.

established model of Northumberland village desertion, as an outsider purchased land and then invested in improving it,[30] although in this case the investor was not a Newcastle businessman but a member of the Northumberland aristocracy. It also differs from the norm in that Grey purchased a large number of freehold properties rather than an entire estate, and because this engrossment did not lead immediately to desertion. It is thus clear that, while general trends can be identified in the county, there are always local conditions which cause important differences in local processes.[31]

Learmouth has a similar history of engrossment followed by landscape reorganisation. In this case, however, the reorganisation occurred some time after the removal of farmsteads from the village and directly resulted in depopulation. The entire township of Learmouth was owned by the Greys of Howick and their predecessors for several centuries,[32] so its engrossment involved the joining of leasehold farms rather than the purchase of freehold properties. The engrossment of Learmouth appears to have been carried out mainly in the eighteenth century,

30. Wrathmell, 'Village depopulation'.
31. Wrathmell, 'Village depopulation'.
32. Vickers, *Northumberland*, pp. 75–6.

although there is some evidence of engrossment prior to 1708, as two of the six farms listed in a rental of that year were in the hands of one man, and later leases describe two of the others as 'those six ffarms com[m]only called the West side of Learmouth'.[33] In 1712 these two farms were themselves engrossed by one Thomas Gregson.[34] From 1719 Anthony Compton, who was an alderman of Berwick-upon-Tweed, began to take leases of Learmouth farms.[35] By 1733 he had acquired all the farms in the township other than the glebe, creating near unity of control.[36] In these leases he is described as 'of Learmouth' for the first time, indicating that he had moved there.[37] He probably built West Learmouth Farm, which first appears on a plan of 1793.[38] In 1778 further dispersal occurred when an agreement enclosed the glebe and abolished some tithes in exchange for land.[39] This land was allotted in the south of the township on some relatively low-quality land,[40] suggesting that the landlord, Henry Grey, was the more powerful party to the agreement. This created Tithe Hill Farm. By 1793 Learmouth consisted of three dispersed farmsteads – the two described above and a third called The Hagg, whose origins are obscure but which certainly existed by 1778 – and the village, which contained approximately eight buildings.[41] In 1799 the township was enclosed, along with several other farms in the Tweedside part of the Howick estate.[42] At this time East Learmouth Farm was created by dividing the township in two. At the same time the village was depopulated and replaced with labourers' cottages at both East and West Learmouth Farms. Later still, between 1842 and 1866, Lightpipehall was constructed, although this appears to have been a private house. Again, this is typical of processes within the county in that an investor, the elder Anthony Compton, engrossed the township, leading to dispersal and probably village shrinkage.[43] In this case, however, the investor was a tenant, not a freeholder. Again, depopulation did not occur immediately after the farms had been moved out of the village but much later, under Anthony Compton's heirs, during a period of estate-wide landscape reorganisation.

We have thus seen that local factors caused settlement desertion to vary greatly in each instance. It has also been observed that settlement dispersal could occur

33. DUSC GRE/X/P80, GRE/X/P72.
34. DUSC GRE/X/P72.
35. DUSC GRE/X/P73, DUSC GRE/X/P73, DUSC GRE/X/P73 1729.
36. DUSC GRE/X/P74.
37. DUSC GRE/X/P74.
38. DUSC GRE/X/P276.
39. DUSC GRE/X/P276.
40. Agricultural Land Classification <http://magic.defra.gov.uk/datadoc/metadata.asp?dataset=2>, accessed 15 August 2012. This area is land classification Grade 3, in contrast to the Grade 2 of the rest of the township.
41. DUSC GRE/X/P276.
42. DUSC GRE/X/P181.
43. Wrathmell, 'Village depopulation'.

before village desertion. This allows the possibility that dispersion could happen without any desertion: a settlement process that has largely been ignored by scholars and yet which can be observed in some of our other case studies. It will be shown that it is in many ways similar to the desertion processes which have been discussed above, further demonstrating the variety of events which the unique local assemblages of actors could create.

Settlement dispersal without village depopulation

Little is known of the process of settlement dispersal without village depopulation nationally, although some reasons for settlement dispersal more generally, such as a desire for privacy or efficiency, probably apply in many cases.[44] Some, such as the farmhouses built on the newly enclosed downs of Berkshire, Wiltshire, Dorset, Hampshire and Sussex following the enclosure of wastes by act of parliament during the Napoleonic Wars, was clearly caused by the expansion of the arable area.[45] A well-understood example is the Salisbury Plain Training Area, where new farmsteads were established in the eighteenth and nineteenth centuries on ground enclosed by act of parliament. They were mostly farmed by large tenant farmers and emerged more rapidly in areas where enclosed land included a larger proportion of former open field.[46] Similar cases of farmstead construction on former common enclosed by act of parliament have been observed in some of our townships. One example is at Learmouth, where land was allotted to Henry Grey in lieu of rights on Wark Common in 1799.[47] As Learmouth township does not directly border Wark Common this land could not be incorporated into either of the two farms there. Instead, a new farmstead was built on the allotment, which was leased as a separate farm called Wark West Common.[48] More examples are to be found at Elsdon. Here the large number of proprietors and the arrangement of the ancient land resulted in many allotments being laid out separately from their farms. Some of these were made into new farms: East and West Hillhead, for example, were built on the allotments for Townhead and William Charlton's tenement respectively; a farm called Colsters was built on one of the allotments for Landshot; yet another, called Loning House, was built on the allotment for Ralph Anderson's lands; and a ruined building on the allotment for The Flatt suggests that this was a separate farm for a short time.[49] Pearson's House is better documented. This was built on an allotment for Burnstones probably between

44. Williamson, *Transformation*, p. 47.
45. Bettey, 'Downlands', p. 42.
46. Brown, 'Post-enclosure farmsteads', p. 123.
47. NRO QRA 63/1.
48. DUSC GRE/X/P79.
49. NRO QRD3; first edition Ordnance Survey map <http://digimap.edina.ac.uk/historicdownloader/ downloader;jsessionid=3C1F1AA442B9D5F501C55A5DA7F2C7DD?execution=e1s1>, accessed 3 April 2011.

Figure 5.2 The remains of Pearson's House, which was built on a detached enclosure allotment after it had been purchased by a wealthy quarry owner from Walbottle, near Newcastle-upon-Tyne.

1766 and 1820, rather than immediately following enclosure. In 1731 Burnstones was owned by Alexander Hall, but it was soon passed to his son Thomas Hall.[50] Thomas Hall sold it to Thomas Pearson on 31 January 1766, and it is probably this Pearson or one of his sons remembered in the name of the farm. Thomas Pearson was neither local nor a farmer. He lived in Newcastle and made his fortune from his quarry at Walbottle.[51] Thomas Pearson died in 1775, leaving the farm to his sons Francis and Thomas to come to them when they turned 21,[52] but both shares were soon sold to Thomas Thornton of Harwood.[53] This suggests that the farm was built between 1766 and 1820, when the first part of it was sold, and probably during the life of Thomas Pearson the elder. The house itself, which was stone-built and contained within a garth, survives as an earthwork. It was very small, containing only two rooms and a byre or shed on its ground floor (Figure 5.2). Such a small house was probably never the home of a gentleman such as Pearson and so was probably tenanted, as is also suggested by the fact that the Pearsons lived in Newcastle or Middlesex.[54] This, therefore, is an example of an outside

50. NRO ZBS/26/2.
51. NRO ZBS/26/2.
52. NRO ZBS/26/2.
53. NRO ZBS/26/2, NRO ZBS/26/2.
54. NRO ZBS/26/2, NRO ZBS/26/2.

investor buying land and creating dispersed settlement, although on a smaller scale than we have so far examined. Loning House has a similar story. A very similar structure to Pearson's House, consisting of two rooms and a byre or shed on the ground floor, it was built on the allotment for Ralph Anderson's lands.[55] It survives better than Pearson's House, but it is still unclear whether or not it had a second floor. This was built by either George Davidson, who bought the property in 1720,[56] or William Goldburn, who bought it in 1773.[57] Davidson is the likely candidate, as he moved to Elsdon between the purchase and his death in 1734.[58] William Goldburn was a butcher from Newcastle,[59] so in either case the construction of the new farm was dependent on the arrival of an outsider.

In some cases, then, detached allotments resulted in settlement dispersal. However, there were many other cases of detached allotments which were not turned into separate farms. It is more accurate to say that in particular circumstances detached allotments could become new farms, in some cases occasioned by the arrival of an outside purchaser. It is clear that expansion of the arable area was not enough on its own to cause settlement dispersal and that other factors were needed. Thus dispersal could also happen in townships where such factors were in operation yet there was no expansion of the arable area.

This was the case at Milfield, where Milfield Hill farmhouse was built between 1777 and 1842.[60] It followed a period of engrossment by one William Mills, as a lease of 1735 says that the property had previously been held by three other people.[61] The construction of the farmstead did not occur immediately after this, as it is not present on a plan of 1777.[62] Enclosure of the area in which the farm stands happened between 1777 and 1789, creating a ring-fenced holding.[63] It is probable that the construction followed this, although it is not possible to determine exactly how soon after enclosure the farmhouse was built. It seems to have been quite a fashionable dwelling, set in a small park planted with exotic trees (Figure 5.3), though little remains now. The roads leading to it were lined with privet (Ligustrum sp.), apple (Malus sp.) and beech (Betula sp.) hedges, none of which are common hedge plants in the area. This case of dispersal also failed to cause

55. NRO QRD3, NRO DT164M.
56. NRO ZBS/26/2.
57. NRO ZBS/26/2.
58. NRO ZBS/26/2.
59. NRO ZBS/26/2.
60. NRO 1356/P26a, NRO DT322S.
61. DUSC GRE/X/P75.
62. NRO 1356/P26a.
63. The 1777 plan shows the area unenclosed, but the 1789 award for the enclosure of the common describes this area as anciently enclosed. It is possible that the 1777 plan shows the allotment to Henry Grey at an enclosure of around this date, as the title says that it is the land belonging to Grey, which would not make sense as a description of an unenclosed area.

Figure 5.3 The remains of the ornamental park around Milfield Hill Farm. Though the farmhouse has not survived, the presence of the park implies that it was an impressive structure.

village desertion. The village actually grew from only six structures to a sizeable settlement containing a chapel, reading room, school and pub, although it may be significant that the other two farms remained in the village and that 'weavers' are recorded in the 1841 census, suggesting that there were employments other than agriculture.[64] Thus, at Milfield dispersal occurred without either expansion of the arable area or depopulation of the village.

The evidence for dispersal is much greater at Longhorsley, but is only available for the northern half (called Bigge's Quarter), which was owned by the earls of Carlisle. A 1719 plan of part of Bigge's Quarter shows only two structures outside the village.[65] By 1773 there were four additional farms in the area shown on the 1719 plan as well as five dispersed sites outside it.[66] Enclosure occurred before 1664, so the dispersed farms were not its direct result. Between 1719 and 1773 ring-fenced farms were created as leases fell in, probably with a significant amount of tenant influence. Many of these had farmsteads constructed on them, but two farms shown in 1773 did not have farmhouses. One was almost certainly farmed from the village, as it is next to it. The other may have been farmed with another holding in Brinkburn Township to the north. The southern half, called Riddle's

64. 1841 census return Ford District <http://search.ancestry.co.uk/search/category.aspx?cat=35>, accessed 26 September 2013.
65. CAS HNP1967/Lambert Plans fos 6v.–6d.
66. CAS C/190/97.

Quarter, has a similar settlement pattern to that shown in Bigge's Quarter in 1773, although, as there is no plan earlier than 1777, it is not possible to determine its dates. Interestingly, Freeholder's Quarter has only two isolated farmsteads depicted on the tithe plan.[67] One of these seems to be on an area of former common called West Moor, and so is similar in origin to some of the Elsdon farms and Wark West Common. The other is Blackpool Farm, which was owned by a Mr John Ogle in 1600. He sold it to John Bolton on 28 July 1600, after which it passed through several generations of the Bolton family until Charles William Bigge purchased it in 1823. As described above (Chapter 3), it is unclear when this became a ring-fenced farm, but it was owned by several wealthy proprietors or enthusiastic improvers. Charles William Bigge's improvement of Bigge's Quarter has already been discussed. George Bolton, who probably owned the farm in 1664, was one of Longhorsley's more substantial freeholders. Finally, John Ogle, while no improver (he opposed the 1664 enclosure), was a wealthy man. Any one of these men may have built the farmstead, but it is probably no coincidence that one of the few dispersed farmsteads at Freeholder's Quarter was owned by such people. Unfortunately the current farmstead is nineteenth century in date and so does not provide physical evidence that might help determine its origins. It is a substantial farm and has ornamental aspects, as its hedgerows contain sycamores, which are unknown elsewhere in Longhorsley. The other farms in Freeholder's Quarter were farmed from the village. This is probably because it has a much more fragmented ownership than either of the other two Longhorsley townships, meaning that the creation of ring-fenced farms required the purchase of a block of adjacent fields rather than simply waiting for leases to fall in, as happened in Bigge's Quarter and probably in Riddle's Quarter (see Chapter 3).

The creation of dispersed settlement, at this date, appears to have been a very varied process. Some new settlements were the result of expansion of the arable area, particularly after parliamentary enclosure, although in at least some cases these were neither a direct nor a necessary result of enclosure. Of these, some were built as a result of the arrival of a wealthy investor. Others were constructed after the formation of ring-fenced farms, as at Longhorsley and Milfield, or indeed Howick and Learmouth. This required enclosure, but did not necessarily result directly from it. Some of these farmsteads are also associated with the arrival of new owners by purchase or inheritance. Others may be the result of estate policy, as at East Learmouth, and perhaps in Bigge's Quarter, in order to attract the 'right' sort of tenant.[68] Dispersed settlements could also result from a desire for privacy or the efficiency of being nearer to the fields. Clearly, then, the same settlement pattern could result from a variety of different circumstances. Enclosure, engrossing and the creation of ring-fenced farms are all necessary circumstances for settlement

67. NRO DT192M.
68. Williamson, Transformation, p. 16.

Figure 5.4 The allotment made to Lord Derwentwater for East and West Whitlees and Leehouses Farms. The fact that all three farms were owned by one person allowed the allotment to be made in one parcel.

dispersal to occur, as a person must be the outright owner of a substantial block of land in order to build on it. However, only in a few cases was the construction of a farm the immediate or necessary outcome of these processes, and it was often delayed until later circumstances caused its creation. Thus, the tendency towards dispersed settlement in this period does not appear overwhelming, and in some cases was even reversed.

The desertion of farmsteads

At both Longhorsley and Elsdon dispersed settlements were deserted during the eighteenth and nineteenth centuries. As we shall see, their original creation was usually the result of engrossment and the subsequent increases in farm size. Before we consider these in detail, however, we will consider contemporary events at Howick, which are particularly interesting because no farmhouse was deserted despite a reduction in the number of farms from five, including the home farm, in the 1770s to two at the beginning of the nineteenth century, though in 1810 another tenanted farm was created, bringing the total to three (Pasture House, Sea Houses and Redstead).[69] This reduction in farm numbers may have been connected with a reorganisation of the estate at inheritance by the second Earl Grey, which, in turn, may have occurred because he was unable to find tenants for such small farms. The reduction was possible without farmstead desertion because some farmhouses were converted to other uses. The home farm seems to have been moved to Pasture House, and the former steward's house and one of the other farmsteads let as private dwellings.[70] Even when Redstead came back in hand in 1818, as a result of the post-Napoleonic War depression,[71] it was kept as a second home farm, and later converted into a model farm.[72]

At Elsdon, in contrast, there were quite high levels of farmstead desertion. Leehouses Farm was shown on the 1731 enclosure plan but not on the 1839 tithe map. The enclosure plan represents it as two structures, suggesting that it was let as two farms, so it is perhaps more a small hamlet than a farmstead. The allotment for it was awarded to one man, John Ratcliffe Lord Derwentwater, along with allotments for the neighbouring East and West Whitlees (Figure 5.4). The fact that all three settlements were owned by one individual would make it possible for them to be united by one tenant, facilitating desertion of all but one of the farmsteads. This appears to have happened to West Whitlees before 1731, as the ancient land of this farm does not have a farmhouse.[73] The remains of Leehouses are quite slight, while East Whitlees is substantial and contains a bastle (Figure 5.5), which may suggest that the largest of the farms was retained. High Field House, which was a single farmstead in 1731, was also abandoned before the tithe plan was drawn.[74] Despite being marked on the plan it is not mentioned in the enclosure award, but it is likely to have been part of a farm called Stichells, which was glebe belonging to Alwinton parish.[75] It appears that a privately owned farm called Yate Cheek was joined to it after 1731.[76] If so, the farmhouse of Yate Cheek may have been retained in preference to High Field House. South Riding was similarly abandoned through engrossment. It was marked on the 1731 plan, but not on the tithe plan.[77] The apportionment shows that it was in the possession of Fenwick Hedley, who also held Middle Riding, next to it. He was tenant under John

69. DUSC GRE/X/P81.
70. DUSC GRE/X/P253, DUSC GRE/X/P12.
71. DUSC GRE/X/P81. Between 1814 and 1819 the farm passed between a series of tenants, each of whom built up arrears before leaving (DUSC GRE/X/P81).
72. DUSC GRE/X/P12.
73. NRO QRD3.
74. NRO QRD3, NRO DT164M.
75. NRO QRD3.
76. NRO QRD3, NRO ZHE/14/3.
77. NRO QRD3, NRO DT164M.

Figure 5.5 The bastle house at East Whitlees, showing that some enclosure of the common is at least late medieval or early modern.

and Thomas Hedley, so in this case the engrossment was carried out by a tenant, not a landlord, although, since all involved share a surname, the arrangement may have been an informal one between relatives.[78] Colsters was also abandoned. It had been built on one of the detached allotments for Landshot between 1731 and 1839.[79] By 1839, however, it had already been joined to East Nook and its farmhouse was probably abandoned shortly afterwards.[80] It had certainly been deserted by 1866, when the Ordnance Survey map marks a small close and a ruined structure. Its remains today are similar to those shown in 1866. The structure is much too small to have been the farmhouse and may have been an outbuilding or even a later field barn. Finally, the 1866 first edition Ordnance Survey map marks a ruined building called the Flatt Fell on the allotment for The Flatt. This structure is also mentioned in late nineteenth-century surveys of the estate.[81] It is not marked on the enclosure plan, so it must have been built and abandoned after enclosure but before 1866. The tithe is no use in this case as it is unlikely to have marked a ruined structure, so its absence could mean that it was either unbuilt or already ruined. Sadly no archaeological traces survive to confirm this. By 1839 the Flatt Fell had been let to Joseph Patterson, who was also the tenant of neighbouring

78. NRO DT164M.
79. NRO QRD3, NRO DT164M.
80. NRO DT164M.
81. NRO ZHE/14/4.

Dunshield,[82] thus providing a further example of engrossing by tenants. In most cases at Elsdon farmstead abandonment seems to have resulted from the engrossing of neighbouring holdings by tenants and smallholders.

Similar processes seem to have operated in Riddle's Quarter at Longhorsley, but without causing as much desertion. However, as the sources for Riddle's Quarter are very sparse it is possible that there was an estate policy in favour of larger farms. Comparison of the 1777 estate plans of Riddle's Quarter and the 1846 tithe plan show that Paxton Farm and Town Farm were joined together during this time. A piece of Paxton Farm was also sold to the owner of the freehold of the neighbouring Whemleyburn Farm, which may suggest reorganisation by the landlord.[83] This did not lead to abandonment, however, as Town Farm was farmed from a house in the village.[84] At the same time North and South Smallbourne (which was a single farm) and West Smallbourne were joined (Figure 5.6).[85] The name of North and South Smallbourne and the presence of two farm buildings here in 1777 suggest that it had been two separate farms (Figure 5.6). Despite these amalgamations, however, all three farmsteads survived until at least 1846.[86] Evidence of desertion does not occur until the 1866 Ordnance Survey map, which does not mark West Smallbourne at all and shows that part of North Smallbourne was ruined and part still standing (Figure 5.6).[87] Both have now been completely destroyed and their ruins ploughed out, so no archaeological traces remain to confirm the dating. So, despite engrossment, farmstead desertion did not occur immediately.

In Bigge's Quarter farmstead desertion did occur, but probably not by engrossment. Some amalgamation did happen as leases fell in or tenants took several farms (see Chapter 3). However, as most of this took place before 1773 there is no evidence to show whether or not it caused farmstead desertion. The only certain instances of farmstead abandonment are those of Matthew and George Dobson's farm, which was removed to facilitate the creation of a mansion and landscape park, and Widow Hume's farm, which was replaced by View Law to its south. In the latter case the change in location was made by amalgamating Widow Hume's lands with those of Henry Kirsop, which had previously been farmed from the village.[88] Both of these cases seem to have been part of a major reorganisation of the farm boundaries probably carried out by Charles William Bigge.[89] During this process the number of farms was reduced from ten to five (plus the mansion

82. NRO DT164M.
83. NRO DT164M, NRO ZHE/14/13.
84. NRO 1255/1.
85. NRO 1255/1.
86. NRO DT391M.
87. First edition Ordnance Survey map <http://digimap.edina.ac.uk/historicdownloader/downloade r;jsessionid=876F0BBEC797212BF40AFCBBF5ACB8A9?execution=e1s1>, accessed 6 June 2011.
88. CAS C/190/97, NRO DT43M.
89. CAS N/13/15.

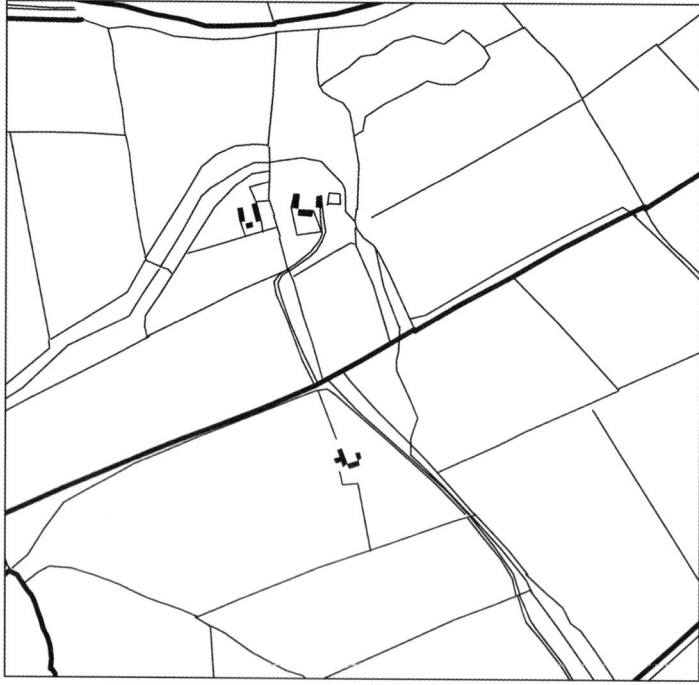

1777

1866

N

0   2.5   5
              km

———— Field boundaries

Figure 5.6 The three Smallbourne farmhouses in Riddle's Quarter, Longhorsely, were abandoned between 1777 and 1866 following the joining of the farms associated with them.

and landscape park), so it is interesting that the number of desertions is so few.[90] This is the case partly because some of the 1773 farms did not have farmsteads and also because two 1773 farmsteads were retained for other purposes.[91]

All of these desertions involve an increase in farm size, but it is also true that many increases in farm size at Howick and Longhorsley did not result in desertion. An increase in farm size is essentially engrossing, so the processes behind farmstead desertion are similar to those which cause village desertion. To some extent, larger farms were desirable during this period because of their greater efficiency or ability to attract more substantial tenants, who could stock large farms and would not fall into arrears.[92] There were also some contemporary authorities, notably Arthur Young, who advocated larger farms.[93] On the other hand, some factors were working to balance out the increases in farm size, such as the difficulty in finding tenants who had the capital to stock large farms.[94] In addition, while Young was advocating large farms, others were of the opinion that there was an upper limit in size above which increase was counterproductive.[95] Whether the balance of these opposing forces caused a significant change in the social structure of rural England is controversial and lies beyond the scope of this book.[96] Nonetheless, there does appear to have been a gradual growth in farm size nationally.[97] Certain periods, such as the late seventeenth century[98] or Parliamentary enclosure,[99] have been suggested to contain more engrossment than others, but both periods have been strongly criticised.[100] As this happened at a time when other factors were causing settlement *dispersal*, the engrossment of dispersed farms did not have as much impact on settlement patterns as it might have done.

Engrossment resulted from many different processes. At Howick and Longhorsley it may have been estate policy at various times, the effects of which

90. CAS C/190/97, NRO DT43M.
91. NRO DT43M.
92. G.E. Mingay, 'The size of farms in the eighteenth century', *Economic History Review*, 14 (1962), pp. 471–5; Williamson, *Transformation*, pp. 16–17.
93. J.V. Beckett, 'The debate over farm sizes in eighteenth- and nineteenth-century England', *Agricultural History*, 57 (1983), p. 312.
94. Mingay, 'The size of farms', pp. 475–7.
95. Beckett, 'Debate over farm sizes'.
96. D.E. Ginter, 'Measuring the decline of the small landowner', in B.A. Holderness and M.E. Turner (eds), *Land, labour and agriculture 1700–1920: essays for Gordon Mingay* (London, 1991) pp. 27–48.
97. Williamson, Transformation, pp. 16–17; Mingay, 'The size of farms', p. 309; D. Grigg, 'Farm size in England and Wales, from early Victorian times to the present', Agricultural History Review, 35 (1987), p. 181.
98. Mingay, 'The size of farms', pp. 480–87.
99. J.L. Hammond and B. Hammond, *The village labourer 1760–1832: a study of the government of England before the Reform Bill* (1911; Stroud, 1995), pp. 97–105.
100. Ginter, 'Measuring the decline'.

have been observed elsewhere.[101] At Elsdon, in contrast, without a single powerful landlord, the process was carried out by tenants and smallholders. The effect of agricultural depression may also have caused engrossment, as fewer tenants could be found. Similar processes occurred in Sussex,[102] may have happened at Riddle's Quarter and certainly happened at Howick, when Redstead went in hand after the Napoleonic War, although in both cases the farm buildings were kept. All the cases of farmhouses being kept despite being separated from their lands occur within large estates, perhaps because the greater administrative apparatus of an estate was able to find new uses for these structures, such as letting them as dwellings or workshops, more easily than were the smaller landowners at Elsdon.

The desertion of these farmsteads is part of the almost constantly changing settlement pattern that we have observed throughout the post-medieval period at each of our townships. We have divided these processes into the depopulation of villages, the creation of dispersed settlements and the desertion of dispersed settlements, although there are great similarities between all three, despite their outcomes. These processes also cover all possible changes other than the creation of nucleated settlements, so perhaps this is a period of general change rather than specific trajectories.

At both Howick and Learmouth the general circumstances fit established narratives reasonably well, in that wealthy outsiders invested in engrossing farms formerly worked from the village and built isolated farmsteads.[103] However, they also differ in particular local respects, such as the fact that the desertion of the villages is delayed in both cases and that Edward Grey of Howick was a member of an established family. Neither of these are particularly serious differences.[104] However, they do show the effect of particular local circumstances upon the process. More importantly still, we have observed that in other combinations of circumstances similar processes of engrossment could lead to settlement dispersal without village desertion and to the desertion of isolated farmsteads, again as a result of the particular combination of people and things present in each township.

As with farm consolidation and land-use change, which are often thought of as integral aspects of enclosure, settlement dispersal is in fact a complex and contingent process. Agricultural improvement is also thought to be a result of enclosure, but, as will be demonstrated in the next chapter, is just as complicated as settlement dispersal.

101. J.R. Wordie, 'Social change on the Leveson-Gower estates, 1714–1832', *Economic History Review*, 27 (1974), pp. 593–609.
102. J.A. Sheppard, 'Small farms in a Sussex weald parish 1800–1860', *Agricultural History Review*, 40 (1992), pp. 127–41.
103. Wrathmell, 'Village depopulation'; Dixon, 'Deserted villages of Northumberland'.
104. Cf. Wrathmell, 'Village depopulation'.

6

Adopting new technology
and methods

Agricultural improvement, as a unified movement, appears to begin in the sixteenth or seventeenth centuries, with the widespread adoption of convertible husbandry, water meadows and land draining.[1] It is, however, unclear how effective these techniques were.[2] The 'classic' agricultural revolution began during the mid-eighteenth century and continued into the early nineteenth century. This period saw a great flowering of agricultural literature and much experimentation with livestock breeding, machines, rotations and other technologies. It is clear, too, that economic factors contributed. It is possible, for instance, that increasing rents in Scotland during the eighteenth and early nineteenth centuries is related to increasing improvement during this time.[3] On a national scale is it quite likely that increasing conversion of pasture to arable during the Napoleonic Wars was fuelled by higher grain prices.[4] However, alongside economics was the development of farming as a fashionable pursuit in which agricultural technology gained symbolic or social value.[5] Improvements which offered no monetary return were occasionally made[6] and contemporary literature often presented the adoption of improved agriculture as a moral imperative.[7] Improvement in agriculture was thus seen as an index of civilisation by contemporaries, making its practice a patriotic duty. The use of improved methods, then, demonstrated subscription to these beliefs.[8] The fact that the people who participated in this fashion for improvement were wealthy gentry or aristocracy supports the idea, popular in the earliest scholarship,

1. Kerridge, The agricultural revolution.
2. Overton, Agricultural revolution in England.
3. M. Johnstone, 'Farm rents and improvement: East Lothian and Lanarkshire, 1670–1830', Agricultural History Review, 57 (2009), pp. 43–4.
4. Prince, 'Changing rural landscape', p. 30.
5. Tarlow, Improvement.
6. Tarlow, Improvement, pp. 52–4.
7. E.g. A. Young, A six weeks tour through the southern counties of England and Wales (Edinburgh, 1772), p. ix.
8. Tarlow, Improvement, p. 35.

that the agricultural revolution was led by a small group of aristocratic or gentry improvers.[9] In its simplest form this idea is clearly incorrect, however, as, for instance, the advice given by farming manuals was often inaccurate or even wrong, and, as we have already seen, the tenantry were more than able to drive change.[10] It is possible that, while perhaps not being the sole or even the most significant force behind improvement, a genuine effort on the part of certain aristocrats may have created an atmosphere favourable to improvement in their local area;[11] but it is clear that the tenantry were at least as important as the landlords as, for instance, improvement occurred on some farms of the Holkham estate in Norfolk before attempts were made by the estate to enforce such practices.[12]

The end of the Napoleonic War in 1815 led to a depression which lasted into the 1830s and may have slowed improvement. The situation improved from the 1830s onwards and, indeed, the 1840s and 1850s were a favourable time for arable agriculture. At this time a new phase of the agricultural revolution, known as 'high farming', began. This movement stressed the importance of scientific practice in agriculture and relied heavily upon manure inputs for maintaining fertility. This manure was imported from outside the farm itself, coprolites and guano being particularly important. However, depression set in again in 1873, when grain prices dropped. Farming did not recover from this depression until 1914, bringing us to the end of our period of interest.

We have seen, then, that various different things – prices, fashion, estate policies, landlords' attitudes, tenants' efforts and probably many others – are implicated in the narrative of agricultural improvement and influenced the local uptake of improvements. These may be observed directly in our townships, and as a result we may develop a much more subtle and complex understanding of individual improvement events than has hitherto been possible. It will be shown that improvement occurred only when a large number of people and things came together, but these were never exactly the same in any two cases. Thus, it is not possible to identify a set of factors which *necessarily* led to improvement. This is best understood one township at a time.

Howick

Howick has particularly rich documentation, allowing a window onto many aspects of its improvement. It shows that, on the home farm, improvement occurred in bursts of intensive activity separated by periods of reduced innovation. The leasehold farms show similar bursts of activity, but are less well documented. A variety of reasons

9.   Prothero, *English farming*, p. 161.
10.   Overton, *Agricultural revolution in England*, p. 4.
11.   D. Brown, 'Reassessing the influence of the aristocratic improver: the example of the fifth duke of Bedford (1765–1802)', *Agricultural History Review*, 47 (1999), pp. 182–95.
12.   S. Wade-Martins and T. Williamson, 'The development of the lease and its role in agricultural improvement in East Anglia, 1660–1870', *Agricultural History Review*, 46 (1998), pp.127–41.

embodying the factors discussed above, and many others, lie behind this sporadic activity, but it was usually associated with the arrival of a new owner or tenant.

The eighteenth century

Little can be said about eighteenth-century improvement at Howick. However, the fact that several leases were granted in 1712[13] may imply that the estate was reorganised at this time, perhaps because of Sir Henry Grey's inheritance of Howick in 1710.[14] More formal control over the estate, through the use of written leases, is itself a form of improvement. A description of two cows bred and fattened at Howick in Culley's *Observations on Livestock* shows another type of improvement.[15] This describes two cows belonging to Sir Henry Grey, son of the Henry Grey who introduced the leases, suggesting that he was using the farm to demonstrate his knowledge of agriculture to his peers and thus following fashion.

The early nineteenth century

From 1804 there was a great deal of activity relating to farming at Howick that constituted a distinct phase in its improvement. Some changes were to administrative practice. Several forms were introduced for the information of Charles Grey, to whom the estates had passed. Of these the most numerous are the rentals and farm returns. The former give the amount of rent due from, and paid by, each tenant every six months. The latter were completed fortnightly, and give details of the purchase and sale of stock, use of different types of grain and the labour performed by each worker on each day.[16] This represents a greater amount of attention paid to farm and estate management. In addition to being an improvement in themselves, they provide a source for tracking improvement at Howick. The farm returns show considerable building work between 1804 and 1808,[17] as they recorded labourers and hinds transporting or breaking stones.[18] Some of this construction may relate to drainage or field boundary construction, although some activities, such as thatching and 'assisting the mason', are certainly connected with the construction of farm buildings.[19] Some of this work may be connected with the division of the farm into two halves to allow South Side Farm to be let to a tenant, as it was by 1810.[20] It is likely that this prompted refurbishment of the farmhouse.

13. DUSC GRE/X/P72.
14. Bateson, *Northumberland*, p. 352.
15. DUSC GRE/X/P302/100.
16. DUSC GRE/X/P81, DUSC GRE/X/P7–12.
17. DUSC GRE/X/P7.
18. 'Hinds' were farm workers hired on a year-long contract at the end of which they were paid a lump sum. This was in contrast to 'labourers' who were paid an hourly wage which they received at the end of the week.
19. E.g. DUSC GRE/X/P7, DUSC GRE/X/P7.
20. DUSC GRE/X/P81.

There is also evidence for modernisation of agricultural practice, although the absence of evidence for eighteenth-century practices makes it difficult to judge its scale. For instance, drainage is mentioned many times in farm returns between 1804 and 1808, but less so afterwards.[21] Some innovation and experimentation in crop production also occurred. For example, a threshing machine was used from 1804, and harrowing is also mentioned in the same year.[22] It is possible that these techniques had been in use before the 1804 return, although the threshing machine was a recent innovation.[23] Seed drills were first mentioned in 1814.[24] Experimentation with crop varieties is also revealed, as some are mentioned only once and occupied only a small amount of labour. The earliest example is cabbage, mentioned in the return of 5 April 1805.[25] Buckwheat is also mentioned in this year, and again in 1809, but occupied only one person for one day in each case.[26] Another case occurred in 1814, as a document of 24 December gives the results of an experiment with different types of turnips.[27] 'Swedish', 'white' and 'red top' turnips were all tried, four perches of each being planted. White gave the greatest overall yield but produced fewer tops than the other two. Of these, red top produced both greater root and top yields than Swedish.[28] Innovation seems to have continued into the 1820s, with ribbing mentioned in 1820[29] and seaweed tried as a fertiliser in 1827;[30] it must have been rejected, however, as it was not mentioned again until 1837.[31]

There appears, therefore, to have been a major period of improvement in the early decades of the nineteenth century. This comprised investment in building, drainage, experimentation, new crops and new machines. It coincides with the inheritance of the estate by Charles Grey (later the second earl) in 1808,[32] as he had probably begun to manage the estate during the later years of his uncle, Henry Grey's ownership.[33] The earliest changes are also contemporary with the rise of grain prices due to the Napoleonic Wars, although experimentation continued well after the depression following their end.

21. DUSC GRE/X/P7.
22. DUSC GRE/X/P7.
23. N. Harvey, A history of farm buildings in England and Wales (Newton Abbot, 1970), p. 93.
24. DUSC GRE/X/P8.
25. DUSC GRE/X/P7.
26. DUSC GRE/X/P7.
27. DUSC GRE/X/P111.
28. DUSC GRE/X/P111.
29. DUSC GRE/X/P9.
30. DUSC GRE/X/P9.
31. DUSC GRE/X/P10.
32. Bateson, Northumberland, p. 352.
33. Smith, Lord Grey, p. 136.

There was much less activity during the 1830s, which may be attributable to Grey's term as prime minister[34] or to the economic downturn following the end of the Napoleonic Wars. From this time innovation slackened off and the only new introductions were mechanical grubbing in 1835 and oil cake cattle fodder in 1832.[35] Building and draining also occurred at a much lower level than during the first decade of the nineteenth century.[36]

This first phase of improvement appears to have been strongly connected with the life of Charles Grey. It does, however, involve many other factors. For example, this wave of improvement occurred at the same time as a rise in prices at the start of the Napoleonic Wars, which may have provided capital for some improvements. However, improvement did continue after the end of the war in 1815, so it may also have been related to the growing fashion for agricultural improvement in this period, although this was associated more with Tories than with Whigs.[37] Finally, it fits in with national trends in farming technology, as the period is one of innovation nationally and most of the technology discussed here was new at the time.

The 1840s and 1850s

Nationally, and at Howick, the 1840s mark a period of renewed investment and innovation.[38] The improvements carried out at Howick were probably the initiative of Frederick Grey, the third son of Charles Grey, who seems to have run the estate on behalf of his brother, Henry, the third Earl Grey.[39] As before, administration became more complex, and a large number of documents date to this period.[40] These include the 'Building' and 'Draining' Books,[41] which recorded investment in the leasehold farms, and the 'Cultivation Returns', which reported the crops grown by each tenant.[42] At the same time the farm returns began to be filled in separately for Redstead and Pasture House Farms, and the crops harvested from each field of the home farm were recorded in notebooks.[43]

---

34. Smith, Lord Grey, p. 258.
35. DUSC GRE/X/P9, DUSC GRE/X/P9.
36. DUSC GRE/X/P9.
37. D. Gent, 'The seventh earl of Carlisle and the Castle Howard estate: whiggery, religion and improvement, 1830–1864', Yorkshire Archaeological Journal, 82 (2010), pp. 315–41.
38. Williamson, Transformation, p. 140.
39. This is demonstrated by the fact that many letters in the estate correspondence are signed by or addressed to him: e.g. DUSC GRE/X/P125/10, in which William Burn, steward at Redstead, informs Grey of the methods of cattle feeding being used and the fact that he is running out of linseed, and asks for Grey's approval for changes to the labourers' wages.
40. E.g. DUSC GRE/X/V101, DSUC GRE/X/V102–3.
41. DUSC GRE/X/V101, DSUC GRE/X/V102–3.
42. GRE/X/P271.
43. DUSC GRE/X/P7–12, DUSC GRE/X/V111 1845–1881.

Figure 6.1 The Grey arms on a cottage in Howick village which was built during the early 1840s, at the beginning of the second phase of improvement.

In this period the earliest improvement was the rebuilding of many of the village cottages. Plans of these, drawn around 1841, survive, as do most of the buildings.[44] These structures are quite grand, reflecting the increasing importance of estate villages as status symbols in the mid-nineteenth century.[45] One cottage bears the Grey badge (Figure 6.1). They are well equipped with piggeries, privies and ashpits in yards behind them (Figure 6.2).[46] The importance of the aesthetics of the village is rendered by tenancy agreements which survive from 1846.[47] These required that no rubbish be left in the streets, that the gardens were kept neat and that the windows were repaired and cleaned.[48] They also sought to control the tenants morally, requiring that the sexes were separated in the bedrooms on the upper floors and that no lodgers or dogs were kept.[49] The prohibition against dogs was probably intended to prevent poaching.

The village cottages were not the only construction work performed at Howick during this time. Between 1846 and 1858 accounts and other documents

44. DUSC GRE/X/P277.
45. Williamson, *Transformation*, pp. 162–81.
46. DUSC GRE/X/P277.
47. DUSC GRE/X/P69 1846.
48. DUSC GRE/X/P69 1846.
49. DUSC GRE/X/P69 1846.

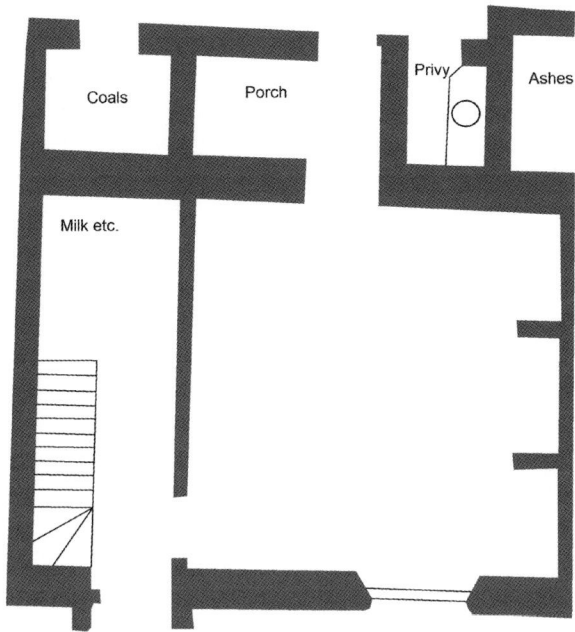

Figure 6.2 A plan of one of the 1840s cottages at Howick village, based on DUSC GRE/X/ P277. It is well equipped with an ash-pit, privy and coal shed, and each pair shared a piggery (not shown on the plan).

show that building work was performed at several farms on the Grey estates. This appears to have been an estate-wide programme,[50] but included both Howick farms. Much work was done at Redstead, which may have been almost completely reconstructed, and appears much larger on the 1866 Ordnance Survey map than on earlier plans (Figure 6.3). Various different types of building were built or refurbished during this time. The cattle lodge, offices and cottages are mentioned in 1846.[51] In 1847 the liquid manure tanks and stables were repaired or built, and a weighing machine and turnip cutter installed at the cattle lodge. In 1855 the piggeries, manure shed, turnip shed, cattle lodge and offices all received attention.[52] It appears that Redstead was being developed into a 'model farm' to be used for display and experimentation rather than profitable agriculture. This is clearly shown by an 1856 insurance policy. At Pasture House it lists four cottages, a large stable with hay house, two turnip houses, one slaughter house, one cow byre, one loose house, a corn barn, two hovels, a granary over the stable, a cart shed, piggeries, a poultry house and a steam engine and boiler house, while at Redstead there was the farmhouse and

50. E.g. DUSC GRE/X/P182.
51. DUSC GRE/X/P233.
52. DUSC GRE/X/P182.

1759

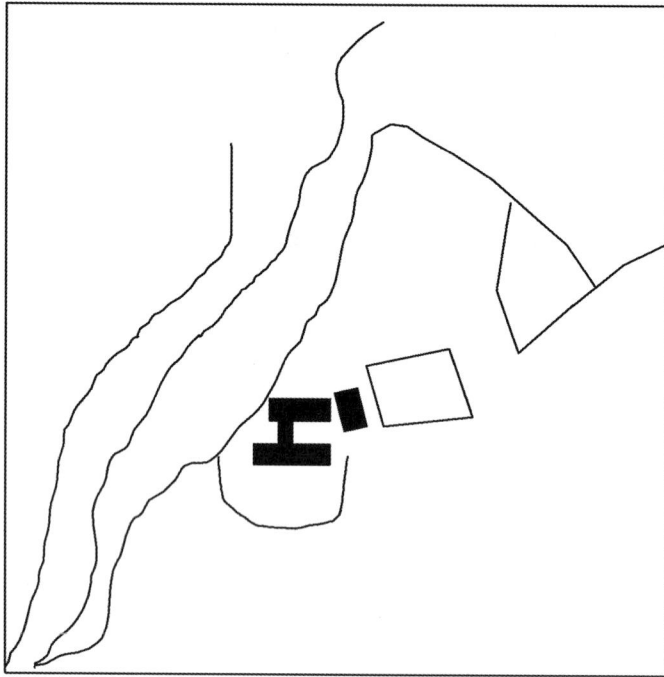

1866

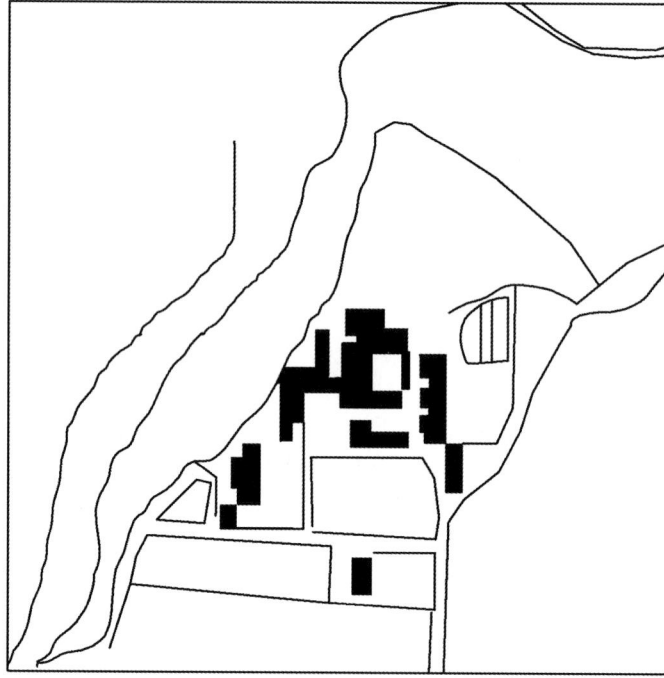

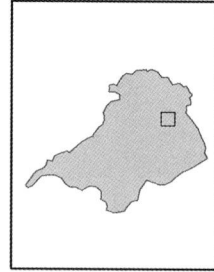

N

0   50   100
              m

Figure 6.3 The farm at Redstead, Howick, was enlarged between the 1759 plan (DUSC GRE/X/P276) and the 1866 Ordnance Survey map in order to make it into a model farm.

Figure 6.4 Ornamental plantations near Redstead, Howick. These further suggest that the farm was at least partly for show.

granary, four cottages, two stables with a hay house and harness room, a cart shed, a granary, a large feeding house, a steaming house, a fodder house with machinery lofts, two implement houses, a liquid manure pump, a saw mill shed with an engine house and three cottages detached from the main building.[53] This shows that Redstead not only had more buildings overall but also had a greater variety of specialist buildings, suggesting an experimental farm. Further evidence that it was a model farm comes from the rearrangement of its fields to create a neater pattern and the planting of several plantations to enhance its aesthetic qualities (Figure 6.4).

In addition to building, investment was made in draining. The farm returns record substantial drainage-related activities from 15 April 1842 onwards.[54] The first references to drainage tiles occur during this time, as the return of 10 June 1842 mentions 'leading pipes from ship',[55] while one of December 1843 records 'laying down tiles at middle pasture field'.[56] The greater bureaucracy at this time means that there are additional sources for drainage. The 'Draining Books' recorded all draining on the Grey estates and include entries for Howick from 1840 to 1886. Other farms also feature, showing that, like building, draining was an estate-wide policy.[57] After 1858 national government played a role in the improvement of

53. DUSC GRE/X/P254.
54. DUSC GRE/X/P11.
55. DUSC GRE/X/P11.
56. DUSC GRE/X/P11.
57. DUSC GRE/X/V102–3.

Howick, as a Lands Improvement Company loan of £1487 15s 7d was acquired to allow further draining across the whole estate, including Howick.[58]

Experimentation with new crops, husbandry practices and manures also recommenced in the mid-nineteenth century. The earliest indications are records of bone dust and nitrate of soda in a farm return of 27 May 1842.[59] Bone later became common, but nitrate of soda must have been a failed experiment, as it does not appear again. Seaweed, which had been tried and rejected early in the nineteenth century, became common from 1843,[60] and guano, which was first mentioned in a report on an experiment of 1845,[61] became common from 1847.[62] Finally, liquid manure is first mentioned in the farm return for 25 February 1848 and was frequently used later.[63] Experiments were conducted to test different types of fertiliser and application methods. For instance, an experiment was carried out in 1846 to test the effect of bones, acid and charcoal; guano, lime and soil; charcoal dust; and 'Muspratt's' on a grain crop. 'Muspratt's' contents are unknown but it must have been a creation of a Liverpool chemical manufacturer of the same name. A control, on which no manure was applied, was also used. The highest yielding was guano, and the lowest the control, although the differences between them were not great.[64]

Innovations were also made in cattle feeding from the 1840s onwards. Little evidence is available for cattle feeding before this time other than references to mangold wurzel and cattle cake in the farm returns of the 1820s and 1830s. From the 1840s there is a huge increase in information as cattle feeding became more scientific. The earliest indication is a group of documents of 1846 which had been filed together.[65] Three documents are descriptions of cattle feeding on farms owned by Lord Prudhoe written by Mr Marshall, Mr Walker and Mr Thomas, who appear to have been bailiffs or stewards. This shows Grey and his employees seeking out new methods of cattle feeding. The procedure is quite complex, including feeding of mixtures of linseed, straw and corn that were measured out, cooked and fed at specified times, and shows the amount of attention paid to improved agriculture at Howick during this period. Frederick Grey appears to have been keen to share knowledge gained from experiments, as he responded to a questionnaire on cattle and sheep feeding sent to him in 1852.[66] In this he mentions, among other things, that he had had success with feeding in boxes,

58. DUSC GRE/X/P343.
59. DUSC GRE/X/P11.
60. DUSC GRE/X/P11.
61. DUSC GRE/X/P261.
62. DUSC GRE/X/P12.
63. DUSC GRE/X/P12.
64. DUSC GRE/X/P200/5.
65. DUSC GRE/X/P125/10.
66. DUSC GRE/X/P186.

but that he preferred stalls for collecting manure, and that experiments had been carried out with a variety of foodstuffs in 1847 and 1848 in which it was found that there was no advantage in cooking fodder. Cooking was dispensed with from that time on as a result.[67]

There is some evidence of communication between Frederick Grey and his land agent on improvements which he had read or heard about. One folder of papers contains cuttings from agricultural journals which had been sent to someone in the estate office.[68] Most of these were from the *North British Agriculturalist* and included articles on 'The Development of the Sources of Ammonia and its Extended Application as a Manure' by Thomas Anderson, Chemist to the Highland Agricultural Society and a 'Report on the Use of the Grubber' by Mr James Porter, Land-Steward at Monymusk, Aberdeenshire.[69] Interestingly, a grubber is mentioned in both inventories and farm returns, which shows that the articles were chosen to be of particular relevance to the farm.[70]

The mid-nineteenth century at Howick home farm was a period of improved agriculture, beginning with the inheritance of the estate by the sons of the second earl. This period involved experimentation, building, drainage, more intensive administration, new methods of animal husbandry, new machines and rearrangement of the farms. An increased volume of documentation allows an even better understanding of the factors governing the introduction of the improvements to Howick home farm. As before, the fact that the changes follow inheritance suggests that they were due to a new owner, Frederick Grey, bringing new ideas regarding estate management. He was clearly responding to fashion as well as profit, as the architectural embellishments of the cottages and the creation of the model farm at Redstead demonstrate. The influence of the peers to whom this display was directed is also apparent from Frederick's correspondence with neighbours on cattle feeding.[71] The political views of his colleagues may also have been significant, as the Whigs were losing the urban associations that they had had during the time of the second earl, leading some to put more effort into their estates.[72]

The tenants of Sea Houses were also involved in improvement. There is less evidence, but this is probably because of biases in the sources rather than any actual lack of improvement. In order to understand the context of the improvements at Sea Houses it is necessary to describe some of its rental history. In 1830 a Mr Thompson took the lease of Sea Houses Farm for £250

67. DUSC GRE/X/P186.
68. DUSC GRE/X/P182.
69. DUSC GRE/X/P182.
70. E.g. DUSC GRE/X/P236.
71. DUSC GRE/X/P125/10.
72. Gent, 'Seventh earl of Carlisle'.

per annum.[73] Thompson got into arrears in 1834, but managed to stay until his death in 1853.[74] His executors were then allowed his debts in exchange for the awaygoing crop.[75] From this time Grey was unable to find a tenant and kept the farm in hand until 1855,[76] when it was let to a Mr Aitcheson and his son for £270 per annum.[77] There is little evidence for improvement under Thompson, which is understandable as he was having difficulty paying his rent at all. Nevertheless, some draining was carried out on Middle Field in 1843,[78] and more noted in the crop book at North Camp Hill, West Field and East Moor may also be of this period.[79] When the farm was in hand some investment was made in the offices and house in 1854 and 1855, with the majority in 1855, presumably to prepare the house for the arrival of the new tenant.[80] The buildings book continues to record improvement by Aitcheson up to 1858, mostly on the farm offices.[81] Draining was also performed during the Aitchesons' tenancy, including that of Middle Field, Camp Hill, North Dove Cot, North Banks and Middle Moor.[82] Some of the capital came from the 1857 loan mentioned above.[83] From 1861 the Aitchesons were allowed £30 per annum out of their rent for manures, showing another type of imprrovement.[84]

In this case we can see that the arrival of a new tenant could result in improvement, demonstrating that tenants had some agency. The estate was involved, however, through the provision of capital, and may thus have enabled improvements which tenants could not have conducted alone. It is also clear that economic factors were a strong influence on tenants, as those who struggled to pay their rent rarely made improvements. These economic factors could be both small-scale, relating to the family finances of the tenant, and of much greater magnitude, resulting from national and global trends.

The 1860s and 1870s

Much less improvement happened during the 1860s and 1870s. While many of the fodders and manures that had been introduced earlier continued to be used there is no evidence for new types,[85] and although building is recorded during this

73. DUSC GRE/X/P81.
74. DUSC GRE/X/P81.
75. DUSC GRE/X/P259.
76. DUSC GRE/X/P259.
77. DUSC GRE/X/P259.
78. DUSC GRE/X/V102.
79. DUSC GRE/X/V111.
80. DUSC GRE/X/P182.
81. DUSC GRE/X/V101.
82. DUSC GRE/X/V103.
83. DUSC GRE/X/P343.
84. DUSC GRE/X/P259.
85. E.g. DUSC GRE/X/P107, DUSC GRE/X/P232.

period there is less than before, and it may amount to no more than repairs to existing structures.[86]

Drainage was conducted, although much less than during the 1840s and 1850s. Some drainage was carried out between 1867 and 1868 with the aid of a Lands Improvement Company loan.[87] Further expenditure on drainage is recorded between 1877 and 1886 in a table showing expenditure on drainage and buildings.[88] It may also be significant that the Grey family was in a particularly difficult situation at this time, with high encumbrances on the estate, which may have left them financially vulnerable.[89]

The 1880s and 1890s

The lull in agricultural improvement continued into the 1880s and 1890s, although at least one experiment was carried out. It was performed in 1893 and was a test of nitrate of soda, superphosphate and kinate. It intended to find out how much nitrogen could be profitably be used on a turnip crop, whether potash was necessary and whether sulphate of ammonium was a good source of nitrogen.[90] This, however, was not Grey's initiative. A man called Dr Sommerville, professor of agriculture at Durham College of Science, had written to Albert Grey (the heir apparent of the third earl, who appears to have begun running the farm during the third earl's old age, before inheriting in 1894) to request that the experiment be carried out at his farm.[91] This experiment was performed, although no record of its results is present in the Howick estate papers. On the whole, however, little agricultural improvement was performed. An inventory of 1896 shows a much reduced list of machinery, the only pieces out of the ordinary being the threshing machine, a Massey Harris reaper and a cultivator also made by Massey Harris.[92] The last two items must have been quite new, as Massey Harris was established only in 1891.[93] One innovation made was the letting of the grazing of both the rotation grass and permanent pasture on an annual basis.[94] Catalogues survive for 1893, 1895 and 1899 which give the names of the tenants and their rents.[95] This appears to have been quite profitable. For example, in 1893, the only year in which the total rents were given, fields were let for between £22 5s 5d and £159 15s 7d.[96]

86. DUSC GRE/X/P273, DUSC GRE/X/P212.
87. DUSC GRE/X/P343.
88. DUSC GRE/X/P273, DUSC GRE/X/P212.
89. Durham University Library, *Catalogue Earls Grey*, p. 2.
90. DUSC GRE/X/P232.
91. DUSC GRE/X/P232.
92. DUSC GRE/X/P115.
93. J. Farnworth, *The Massey legacy: a product and company review of Massey, Harris, Massey-Harris, Ferguson and Massey Ferguson* (Ipswich, 1997).
94. DUSC GRE/X/P56, DUSC GRE/X/P112.
95. DUSC GRE/X/P56, DUSC GRE/X/P112.
96. DUSC GRE/X/P56.

This may have been an exceptional year, as the rents per acre were between 29s and 67s in comparison to 19s to 62s and 18s 6d to 60s in 1895 and 1898 respectively.[97] The conditions for renting the pasture survive from 1899 and show how the system operated. The grazing was let until 30 September if in seeds, 30 November if in rotation grass and 31 December if permanent pasture. Grey was responsible for taxes and fees, providing a shepherd, destroying vermin and weeds and mending fences, suggesting that the tenants did very little of the farming themselves.[98] It may be that this system was intended to turn an unprofitable model farm, designed for experimentation and display, into a money-making enterprise.

One aspect of the estate that did interest Albert Grey and his family was the welfare of the labourers in Howick village. Between 1886 and 1892 Albert Grey experimented with different methods for improving the conditions of his workers at Howick and Learmouth. One means attempted was a profit-sharing scheme. In order to do this Low Stead, which is to the south of Howick township, was joined to Pasture House, Redstead and Sea Houses to make a united farm of 1,603 acres.[99] The average expenditure 1866–1886 (specifically, £1180) was taken, £400 added for the rent for Low Stead, and a further £320 as interest at 4 per cent on a nominal capital of £8000, the actual value of the stock being £8275.[100] In other words, the farm was to pay £1900 rent and interest, the surplus to be divided between the workers for the next five or six years.[101] It was found that there was an improvement of profits 1886–1892 compared with 1866–1886, despite a decrease in prices of produce, and the farm managed to pay three bonuses of 6d in the pound. However, they still made an average of £9 less than the rents, but explained that this was due to rabbit damage.[102] Judging from its formal style and detail this document seems to have been prepared for publication or circulation, so there was an element of self-promotion behind the scheme on the part of either Grey or his agent. To assess the success of the exercise, questionnaires were sent to the labourers.[103] In addition to profit sharing, these discuss a cow-keeping scheme, in which a cow could be kept for 3s per week; and a summer half-holiday.[104] In general, the labourers were in favour of these ideas, although some felt that the profit-sharing scheme had had little effect on their enthusiasm for work. This often seems to have been intended to imply that they would have worked hard anyway. In some cases they suggested that a cow would be too much work for single men or women, though they generally believed that it would be an

97. DUSC GRE/X/P112.
98. DUSC GRE/X/P59.
99. DUSC GRE/X/P180.
100. DUSC GRE/X/P180.
101. DUSC GRE/X/P180.
102. DUSC GRE/X/P180.
103. DUSC GRE/X/P180.
104. DUSC GRE/X/P180.

advantage for families.[105] In addition to these experimental schemes, a lecture hall called Copley Hall was constructed in Howick village. This was built in 1883, as a memorandum of this date records that Miss Copley was to finance it, in part, by foregoing an annuity owed to her by Henry Grey.[106] Miss Copley was the sister-in-law of Henry Grey and a noted philanthropist motivated by religious concerns.[107] By 1895 this building included a shop and a reading room and was being enlarged to include a Dairy School, perhaps related to the cow-keeping scheme.[108]

The nature of improvement in this period may reflect the declining fashion for agriculture and perhaps its decreasing profitability, but the personal interest of the fourth earl was also very significant. He was clearly motivated by a sense of moral duty towards his labourers. This may reflect political changes, as, at this time, the Whig Party was transformed into the Liberal Party through an alliance with the Radicals;[109] such a sentiment would not have been held by Whig politicians of the second earl's era.

This discussion suggests that many factors influenced improvement at Howick. These include economics, as both phases of improvement coincide with periods of agricultural prosperity, the first during the Napoleonic Wars and the second during the mid-nineteenth century. In addition, fashion clearly played a role, most obviously in the creation of the model farm and the rebuilding of the estate village, as both phenomena grew in popularity in the middle of the nineteenth century. At the same time, it became more acceptable for Whig politicians to be involved in agriculture. In addition to these influences are the agencies of both landlords and tenants, most obviously in the relationship between periods of change and the arrival of new landowners or tenants. This means that factors which are specific to these people also have a role to play; for example, the burden of Charles Grey's prime ministerial duties seems to have reduced the effort he put into his estate.

Longhorsley

At Longhorsley there is less evidence for improvement than at Howick. This is because estate papers exist only for Bigge's Quarter. Even these go up only to 1807, when the Howards sold their Longhorsley estates.[110] The remainder of the township was owned by smaller estates or owner-occupiers who have not left detailed papers. As a result discussion of these parts is restricted to comparisons with Bigge's Quarter. It is also significant that there was no home farm at

105. DUSC GRE/X/P180.
106. DUSC GRE/X/P263.
107. Durham University Library, *Catalogue of the papers of Miss Elizabeth Mary Copley and some other Copley papers* (2009) <http://endure.dur.ac.uk:8080/fedora/get/UkDhU:EADCatalogue.0137/PDF>, accessed 30 July 2013, p. 1.
108. DUSC GRE/X/P224.
109. G.R. Searl, *The Liberal Party: triumph and disintegration 1886–1929* (Basingstoke, 1992), pp. 16–28.
110. CAS N/13/15.

Longhorsley as there was at Howick. This means that certain improvements, such as the introduction of new crops, that were the choice of the tenant, often remain unrecorded. Nonetheless, it is possible to make some comments regarding improvement at Longhorsley. Owing to differences in the source material it is convenient to divide the discussion into the periods before and after the purchase of the estate by Charles William Bigge.

Howard ownership: pre-1807

There was increasing interest in improvement during the seventeenth and eighteenth centuries. The conditions of leases between 1677 and 1754 show a realisation of the importance of improved agriculture, although it cannot be shown that the conditions were enforced in normal circumstances. The terms of leases in any one year are always the same, suggesting that they were set by the land agent rather than the tenants. The earliest leases, those of 1677 and 1687, contain very few conditions, specifying only that the tenant should maintain the buildings, but would be given timber for this; that the earl would pay all taxes apart from the county keeping tax; and that the tenant was to be allowed an awaygoing crop, but should leave the straw on the premises for his or her successor.[111] This already shows an understanding of manuring, as the straw was left to keep nutrients on the farm. By 1698 another clause had been added preventing the tenant ploughing up the pasture or meadow in the last three years of the term.[112] The leases remained the same until 1719, when more detailed clauses on hedge maintenance were added. These specified the length of hedge to be repaired per year, particular maintenance for newly planted hedges, and that closes separated by a hedge should not be thrown together.[113] The 1719 leases also contained a clause requiring the tenants to spread lime and specifying an amount for each farm, another preventing them selling hay and straw and one requiring them to allow an incoming tenant to scale and dress the meadow.[114] The next set of leases, of 1731, saw similarly significant changes. These included a clause requiring that a proportion of the arable, either a third or a quarter, be fallowed each year, and that this be stirred either three or four times.[115] They also included a requirement that the tenant would not depasture an unusually large number of animals in the final three years of the term and would fence the pasture from Ladyday in that year, and another which prevented the tenant from ploughing up land or putting land down to grass.[116] The final additions to be made to the surviving sequence of

---

111. CAS N/12/6–14, CAS N/12/18.
112. CAS N/12/19–23.
113. CAS N/12/29–34, CAS N/31/2.
114. CAS N/12/29–34, CAS N/31/2.
115. Fallow stirring is the ploughing up of fallow fields in order to destroy weeds; CAS N/12/39–40.
116. CAS N/12/39–40.

leases appear in 1752 and include requirements that all dung produced be used on the premises, that potatoes may not be planted and that the tenant would be responsible for half the cost of any hedge planting.[117] These leases also contained a clause requiring that land should be put down to pasture only after one corn crop, and that lime and manure should be spread first.[118] The only leases to survive after this are of 1753 and 1754 and are identical to the 1752 leases.[119]

These leases appear to show that the Carlisle estate, either because of instructions from Lord Howard himself or at the instigation of one of the land agents, took an increasing interest in improvement. However, it is not possible to show that these terms were actually enforced. It is also impossible to determine whether this interest was motivated by a belief in the 'doctrine' of improvement or simply in order to protect the estate's assets. In addition, the leases do not allow us to assess the extent to which tenants were involved in innovation. This may be determined through the examination of improvements that were actually carried out.

At Bigge's Quarter there is some documentary evidence for the improvement of farm buildings in rental accounts between 1739 and 1741.[120] Few of the entries show what was being built, but some specific types of building are mentioned, including cottages, stables, barns, byres and milkhouses.[121] There seems to have been more building activity at the beginning of the sequence than at the end, which may be due to the arrival of several new tenants. Certainly, much of the work carried out between 1739 and 1741 was on Thomas Pinkney's farm.[122] Pinkney first appears in rentals in 1740,[123] at which time he combined two farms. This may imply that he thought he could profit from farming and may have needed certain improvements to carry out his plans. When his venture failed in 1741 he was replaced by Thomas Hume and Edward Towns.[124] They both had work carried out, which may have completed that begun for Pinkney and also included a milkhouse, barn and byre.[125] Interestingly, Hume and Towns appear in the sections of rentals dealing with building work from 1740, which suggests that the work began before the two entered the farm.[126] There was also much work done on the farms of sitting tenants, including George Dobson (both elder and younger), William Dobson, Lewis Bilton, Ralph Young and Ralph Carnaby, John Dobson and William Bate

117. CAS N/13/2–5.
118. CAS N/13/2–5.
119. CAS N/13/2–5, CAS N/13/6–9.
120. CAS N/113–14.
121. E.g. CAS N/113, CAS N/114.
122. CAS N/113–14.
123. CAS N/114.
124. CAS N/114.
125. CAS N/114.
126. CAS N/114.

between 1739 and 1742,[127] showing that the arrival of new tenants was not the only cause of building work at this time. From 1742 onwards less work was done, perhaps reflecting the more stable tenurial situation from this time to the end of the rentals.[128] It is interesting that Edward Towns, and to a lesser extent George Dobson and Thomas Hume, continue to appear, while other tenants were having less work done.[129] Finally, in 1747, the arrival of Robert Swann seems to have caused work to be carried out on his farm.[130] This suggests that certain tenants were more demanding than others, and that improvements were made at tenants' request rather than at the landlord's initiative. This does not mean that the landlord was without influence in these decisions, as he or she was the provider of capital and almost certainly oversaw the improvements carried out, as they would have affected the value of the farm the next time it came on the rental market.

We can therefore see that improvement under the earls of Carlisle was achieved by both landlord and tenant agency. It has also been shown that it was a response to technological change, as the changes to leases developed in step with understandings of husbandry and not with the arrival of new landlords. These changes were, however, introduced only as the leases came due, and thus the precise timing of their introduction was a result of legal matters.

Charles William Bigge's ownership: post-1807

Major changes were made to the estate following its purchase by Charles William Bigge. As at Howick, these probably represent the new owner bringing in different systems of estate management and farming. Some of these are indisputably improvements, although others may have been seen by contemporaries as steps backwards.

No leases survive from the period of Charles William Bigge's ownership, but 1861 sale particulars give some of their details. These show that four farms were let from year to year, and none for more than 15 years.[131] This is interesting, as 21-year leases, which had been used by Carlisle's agents from at least the seventeenth century, were considered to be better than shorter terms, and much better than leases from year to year, as tenants were more likely to make improvements if they had a secure tenure. The leases from year to year were also by word of mouth and would not have allowed conditions to be easily enforced. As Bigge invested in improvements to boundaries it is unlikely that he made these changes through a disregard for husbandry. It is possible that, if the leases made under Carlisle were a formality to allow Carlisle recourse in the event of a conflict, Bigge decided that

127. CAS N/113–14.
128. CAS N/113–17.
129. CAS N/113–18.
130. CAS N/115.
131. NRO 90421/3.

he could save money by forgoing them. This may have been possible because, as the owner of a small estate on which he lived, he felt that he could monitor his tenants better than could Carlisle and his agents.

Buildings and farm boundaries also show improvement. Unfortunately, after the sale of the estate the records which allowed pre-1807 changes to be linked to individual tenants no longer exist. The plans, however, demonstrate that change continued after 1807. Comparison of the 1773 plan and the tithe plan shows significant differences at most farms.[132] It is impossible to prove that they were carried out under Bigge's ownership, but the fact that little building work is recorded after 1743 suggests that they were. Most of the changes seem to involve joining buildings to create L- or C-shaped structures around a yard. Hedleywood is a good example. In 1773 it consisted of two rectangular structures next to one another which were converted to a single L-shaped structure by 1842 (Figure 6.5). William Bate's farm also follows the pattern, as a group of three rectangular structures was infilled to create a C-shape (Figure 6.5). Finally, the two rectangular buildings of Robert Swan's farm and Fieldhead were both joined to create L-shaped farmhouses (Figure 6.5). Similar changes occur nationally, and were encouraged by farming texts.[133] The yard allowed better collection and preservation of manure, while the buildings were arranged around it in a convenient fashion.[134] It is difficult to speculate on Bigge's motivation for changing the buildings, but it is likely that new buildings increased the value of his farms and, as fashionable structures, would have reflected well on him. It is also important to remember that the improvements to the buildings may have occurred at the request of tenants, although as the improvements occurred at all the farms on the Bigge estate it is perhaps more likely that they were made at Bigge's instigation. Similar changes did not occur at Riddle's Quarter until after 1846, as the tithe plan shows groups of detached buildings similar to those shown in Bigge's Quarter in 1773.[135] The fact that the earlier changes which occurred in Bigge's Quarter stopped at the boundary between the two estates suggests, again, that these were made at the owner's initiative.

It appears, then, that Bigge made changes to the estate after purchasing it, probably for both profit and fashion. Their precise nature was influenced by many different factors. The best example is the reduction in formality of the leases, which was possible because Bigge lived in the township, and could thus keep a closer eye on the tenantry. It is probably also significant that, as a successful banker, Bigge was wealthier than the other landowners at Longhorsley.[136]

132. CAS C/190/97, NRO DT43M.
133. Harvey, *History of farm buildings*, pp. 77–9.
134. Harvey, *History of farm buildings*.
135. NRO DT391M; first edition Ordnance Survey map 1:10,560 1866 <http://digimap.edina.ac.uk/historicdownloader/downloader;jsessionid=5B687A18BE1F83F10AA3ED16E5A62A5C?execution=e1s1>, accessed 12 March 2012.
136. DUSC DPRI/1/1850/B19/1–16.

1773   1842

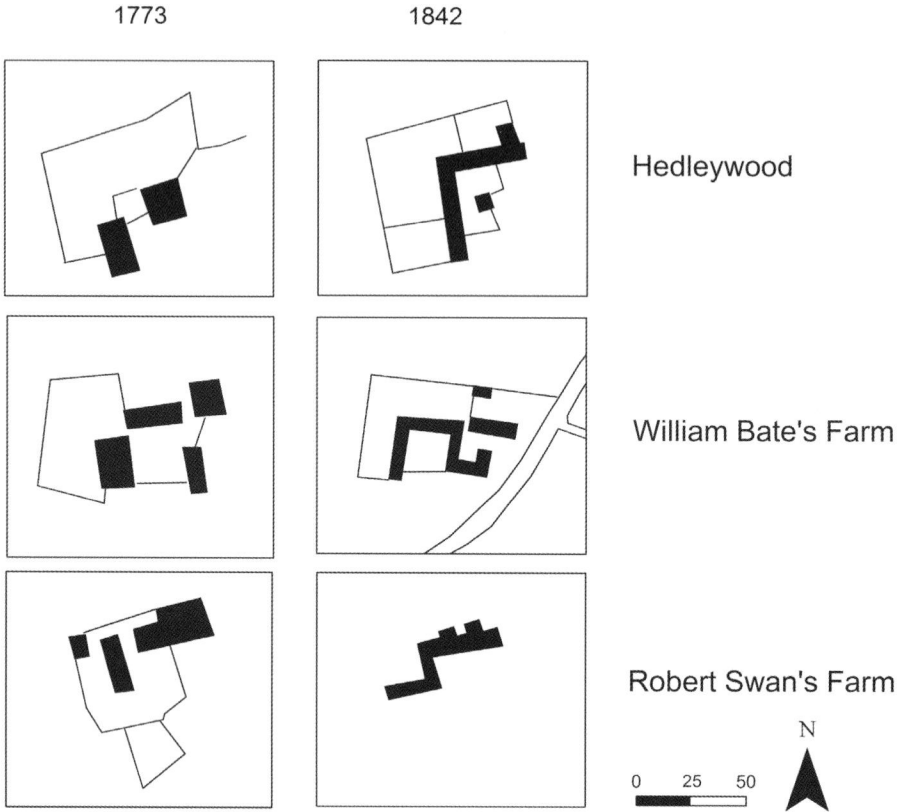

Hedleywood

William Bate's Farm

Robert Swan's Farm

N

0 25 50

Figure 6.5 Between 1773 and 1842 the farms in Bigge's Quarter were significantly improved to create L- or C-shaped structures.

The evidence from Longhorsley appears to confirm that landlords were strongly involved in improvement, both to buildings and to the administration of the estate. The improvements they carried out were affected by their proximity to the farms, fashion and economics, probably in addition to other things invisible in the sources. The tenantry also influenced improvement, clearly requesting, or failing to request, changes to buildings during the period in which the Howards owned Bigge's Quarter.

Elsdon

There is only limited evidence for improvement at Elsdon, but this cannot be taken as evidence for unimproved farming because there is little evidence for husbandry practice in general. The documents that are available are almost all associated with the most substantial landowners, and are thus highly biased. Some comments can be made, however.

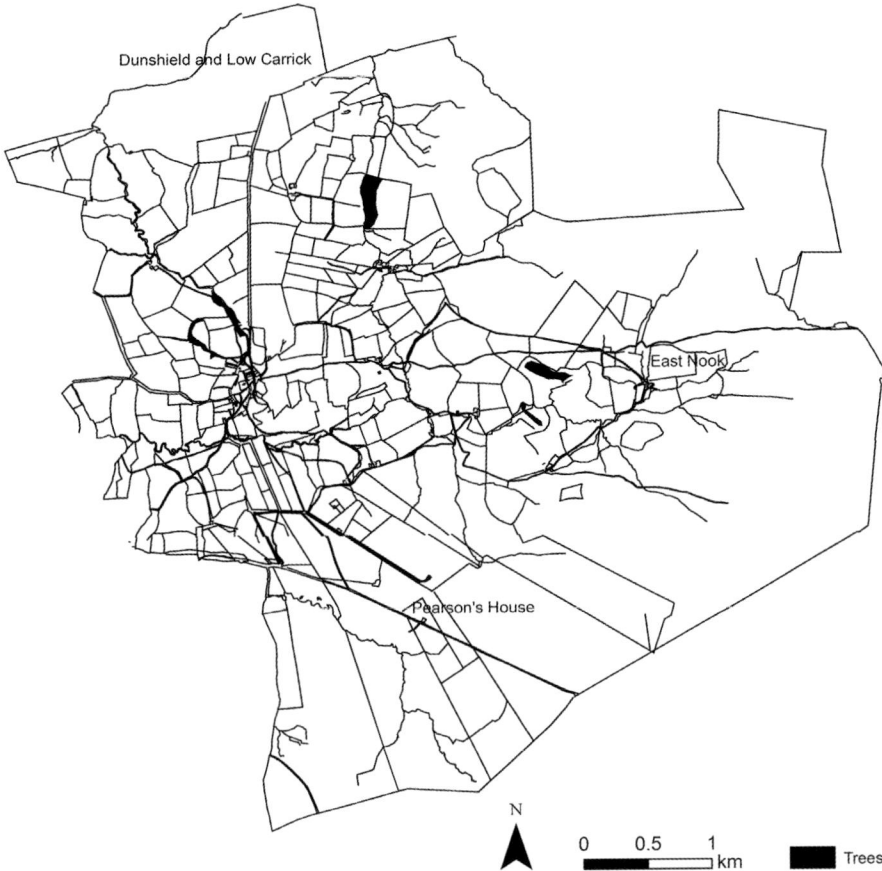

Figure 6.6 The 1866 Ordnance Survey map on which this plan is based shows large open areas on the former Elsdon Common, suggesting that much land had been put down to pasture following enclosure in 1731.

Large areas of the Ordnance Survey map have no field boundaries, which suggests that much of Elsdon township was being used as rough grazing. It was therefore unimproved. This is particularly clear at East Nook, Dunshield and Low Carrick, and Pearson's House (Figure 6.6). In addition, according to the 1840 tithe map, and some later maps,[137] Bainshaw Bog was divided between the glebe of Lowick and Alwinton; however, as no boundary is shown on the Ordnance Survey map it is probable that it functioned as a common used by both their tenants despite being an allotment of the enclosure award. In all cases these were enclosure allotments,[138] so the enclosure of Elsdon failed to cause improvement, and several

137. NRO DT164M, NRO ZHE/14/3.
138. NRO QRD3.

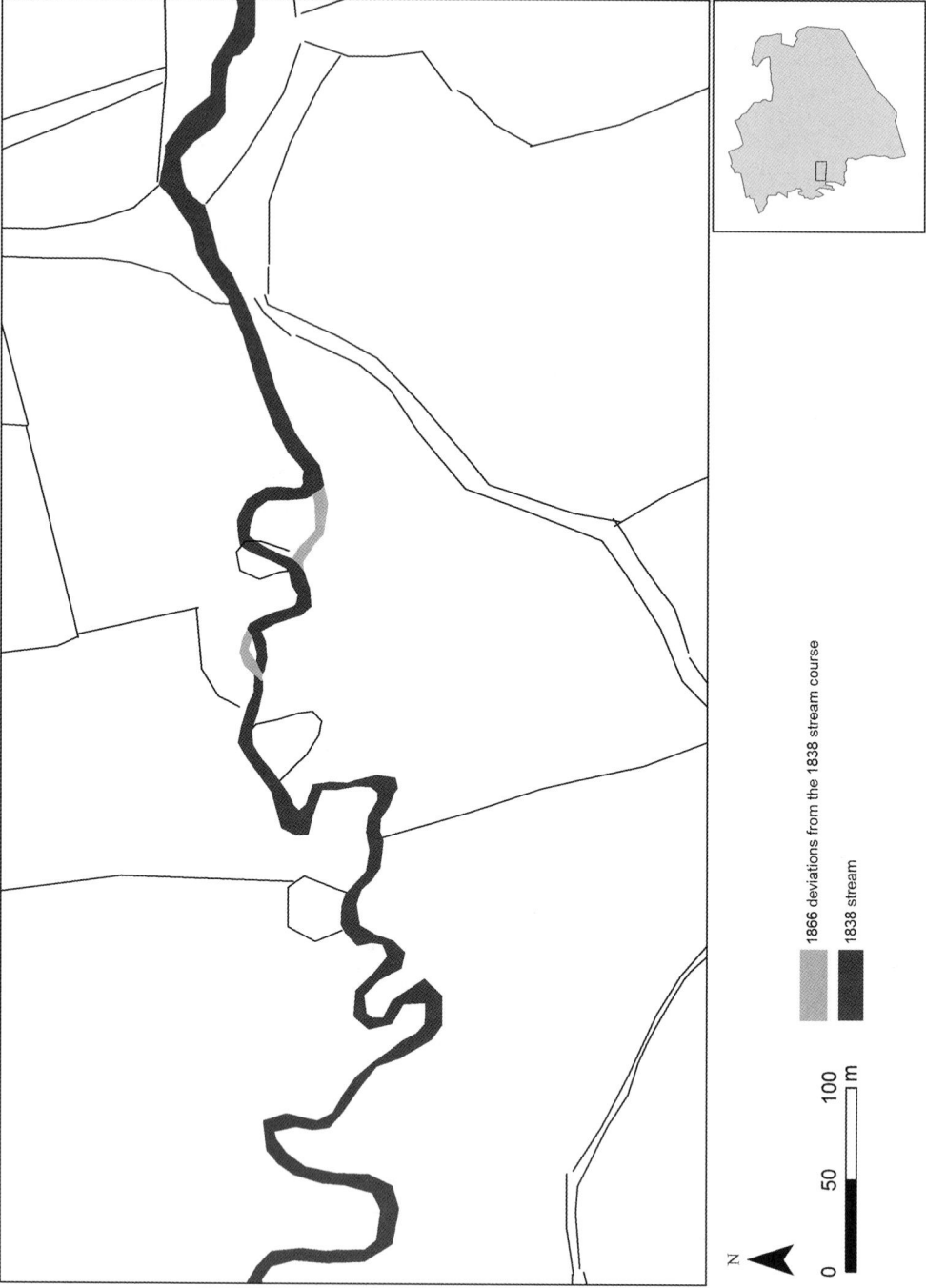

Figure 6.7 This plan shows changes made to a stream called the Monk Burn at Elsdon. The grey lines show the stream in 1838, while the black lines show that two stretches were straightened before the surveying of the 1866 Ordnance Survey map. The Ordnance Survey map also shows several field boundaries which preserve the shapes of other straightened parts of the stream.

documents mention rough pasture. For instance, a report of 1852 regarding the Flatt Fell describes it as partly heath, as does one of 1868.[139] Similarly, an annotated tracing of the Ordnance Survey map of 1873 also marks rough grass in several fields of Cheek Gate Farm. This is in contrast to the other townships examined, where most enclosed land was improved. This may be a product of the poor quality of the land in general or the lack of an overall authority to guide improvement.

On the other hand, there is some sparse evidence for improvement being carried out. The most frequent type was draining. At Cheek Gate Farm, part of the Alwinton glebe, some was performed between the mid-nineteenth century and the 1870s using a Lands Improvement Company loan.[140] Likewise, a tracing of the Ordnance Survey map made around 1866 is annotated to show that £60 9s 4d had been spent on the draining of the south-east corner of the Flatt Fell.[141] In addition, evidence for drainage is available in the form of changes to the course of streams between consecutive maps. An 1838 plan of lands belonging to Thomas Thornton shows watercourses differing from those on the 1866 Ordnance Survey map (Figure 6.7). Similarly, boundaries of several properties on the tithe plan preserve the shapes of meanders in the Monk Burn, which had been straightened before 1840. There are also many very straight watercourses on the Ordnance Survey map, indicating drainage work before 1866; these can be seen at Bainshaw Bog, Pearson's House and Loning House.

Some other types of improvement were used at Elsdon, but evidence for them is yet more restricted. These include a recommendation of C. Seymore Bell to the duke of Northumberland to apply lime to The Flatt,[142] a request from Robert Keith to be allowed to hay the Batt Field in 1899 in order to improve its pasture, and a letter from Mary Whalley, who was a later tenant of the Batt Field, in which she asks for a reduction in rent on the grounds that her leasehold property had been improved 'Owing to the way I fed the cows [one word illegible] cakes, &c &c & laying on manure &c'.[143]

In these cases both landlords and tenants can be seen to be involved in improved husbandry, with landlords providing capital and tenants requesting particular improvements or taking full responsibility for innovations such as the use of oil cake and manures. However, improved methods seem to have been used in limited circumstances in which they were thought to be of greatest utility rather than as a matter of course, as in some other villages. It is likely that many of Elsdon's farms used one or two improved husbandry techniques, but would not have adopted the full range of improvements as contemporary commentators might have preferred.

139. NRO ZHE/14/13.
140. NRO ZHE/14/3.
141. NRO ZHE/14/4.
142. NRO ZHE/14/13.
143. NRO ZBS/25.

Milfield

Milfield has least evidence for improvement. This is because, of the three estates which owned land in Milfield, only the Greys left extensive papers. These have much less material pertaining to Milfield than to the rest of the Howick estate because, for most of the nineteenth century, the tenant of Milfield was also the land agent, and thus was supervised less closely than the others. Some information may, however, be gathered from map regression. On the Greys' property at Milfield plantations were made in the post-enclosure period: many plantations are shown on the Ordnance Survey map of the 1860s, whereas the 1777 map shows an almost treeless environment. Trees on the farm remained the property of the landlord, being reserved to him in leases,[144] so these must have been planted at the direction of either the second or the third Earl Grey. The mechanism by which this occurred is recorded in a lease of 1815, which required that the tenant plant trees on Ewe Hill.[145] Neither of the other two farms saw any tree planting, both being completely treeless on all maps. Clearly neither the Blakes nor the Ordes used their Milfield estates for hunting or timber. Some drainage was also carried out on the Grey estates between 1777 and 1866, as a stream was straightened between these dates. Finally, there is some evidence for improvement of buildings, as an 1803 lease of Milfield Hill required the tenant to build a new farmhouse.[146] In all these cases, however, the landlord seems to have led the improvements. With so little documentation the possibility of tenant improvement cannot be ruled out, however, especially since John and George Grey, who were tenants at Milfield, were occasionally described as improvers.[147]

Learmouth

A better picture of improvement can be gained from Learmouth. There is evidence for extensive drainage at Learmouth in the period after 1793, as changes were made to several watercourses. This included the straightening of a stream on the northern boundary and the alteration of other streams near East and West Learmouth Farms between 1793 and 1843.[148] This may have been a direct result of enclosure, although without more precise dating it is impossible to be certain. It is likely that the intention was to drain the bogs marked on the 1793 map. Certainly no bogs are shown on the tithe map, but their absence may be because the surveyor did not record them. By the 1865 Ordnance Survey map almost all the bog had gone, only English Strother Bog and Marl Bog remaining.

The maps also reveal that many buildings were rebuilt or extended during this period. A byre was added at West Learmouth and unidentified structures were

---

144. DUSC GRE/X/P75, DUSC GRE/X/79, DUSC GRE/X/P35, DUSC GRE/XP35.
145. DUSC GRE/X/79.
146. DUSC GRE/X/P35.
147. Butler, *Memoir of John Grey*, p. 10.
148. DUSC GRE/X/P276, NRO DT286M.

built south and north of East Learmouth. Both of the main farm buildings were significantly altered, being either completely rebuilt or so drastically changed as to be unrecognisable from their ground-plans. There is documentary evidence for building at both farms from the 1830s to the 1850s, which probably includes much of this work. Between the 1830s and the end of the 1840s construction was carried out at both farms. At this time West Learmouth was occupied by a Mr Ralph Compton and East Learmouth by a Mr William Smith. Accounts of 1830–1847 record building expenditure at West Learmouth in 1830 and 1837, then continuously from 1840 to 1846. At East Learmouth it records building from 1841 to 1845.[149] Another account describes building at East Learmouth farmhouse in 1846 and West Learmouth farm offices in 1845.[150] Yet another lists expenditure from 1841 to 1846 at East Learmouth,[151] while another records building at West Learmouth farm offices and gardens in 1845.[152] These documents are quite difficult to interpret, as most are little more than rough notes, so it is unclear whether or not they are complete; it is quite likely that some record only particular types of work. However, they do seem to show that building work was being carried out on a fairly intensive scale in the 1840s. This is probably part of an estate-wide policy, as other Grey-owned farms are mentioned too.[153] Their timing coincides with the inheritance of the Howick estate, of which Learmouth is a part, by the children of the second Earl Grey in 1845.[154] The estate would have provided some capital for the work, but expected either interest or the provision of part of the capital by the tenants, as clauses to this effect exist in contemporary leases.[155] This means that the tenant would choose which work was carried out and, thus, explains why some farms on the Howick estate do not appear in these accounts.

The importance of the tenants is demonstrated by subsequent events. In 1848 Ralph Compton became bankrupt and had to leave East Learmouth.[156] His financial circumstances may have reduced the amount of building which he was able to afford in the years before he left; a report of 1845 says that Mr Compton felt he needed new piggeries but that he could not pay the 6 per cent interest necessary.[157] Although a quote for the proposed work was obtained,[158] it is not clear if it was carried out. It may also be significant that work at East Learmouth ceased in 1846. After Compton left the farm, William Smith surrendered his lease

---

149. DUSC GRE/X/P182.
150. DUSC GRE/X/P233.
151. DUSC GRE/X/P182.
152. DUSC GRE/X/P182.
153. DUSC GRE/X/P182.
154. Smith, *Lord Grey*, p. 324.
155. E.g. DUSC GRE/X/P253, DUSC GRE/X/P221.
156. DUSC GRE/X/P233.
157. DUSC GRE/X/P68.
158. DUSC GRE/X/P123.

of West Learmouth and appears to have moved to East Learmouth in 1849, as this was occupied by a man of the same name.[159] West Learmouth went in hand between 1850 and 1851, and was taken by a Mr John Lumsden in 1851.[160] No further building work is recorded at West Learmouth after Smith had moved out. Much more, in contrast, is recorded at East Learmouth, which may have been even more intensive than under Compton. A list of new buildings on the estate records that, between 1850 and 1856, new stables, a cart shed, a killing house, hovels, a granary, cow byres, piggeries, poultry houses and a building with feeding boxes had been built at East Learmouth. The coach house, riding stables, dog kennels and troughs conducting water to the threshing machine were also restored.[161] An account also records the building of cottages between 1851 and 1857, while another document reveals further expenditure between 1849 and 1852.[162] There are very few records of building after 1857, so it is impossible to comment on later tenants' activities. It is clear, however, that building on the Learmouth farms was strongly influenced by both landlords and tenants. The landlords' policy provided an opportunity for the tenants to have building work carried out. It is also possible that the landlords' agents tried to persuade the tenants to have building work done, as the 1845 report cited above seems to suggest.[163]

There is little evidence for other types of improvement, although a disagreement between the third Earl Grey and a tenant of West Learmouth called William Piper Lumsden shows that some did occur. William Piper Lumsden took the lease of the farm after the death of his father John Lumsden in 1872.[164] Some cropping returns survive for this period showing that most fields were farmed in four- or five-course rotations. This is contrary to the terms of the lease, which required a five-course system, but must have been allowed, as Grey's agent would have been aware of it from the cultivation returns.[165] The four-course system is arguably better as it is more productive, but it may have been too intensive for the Tweedside area. On the best soils on the farm it may have been appropriate and so could be seen as an improvement. There is some indication of further irregularities in William Lumsden's activities, as from November 1879 he began to accrue arrears which he paid off in April 1882. Perhaps because of this he made an agreement with Grey in 1880 that for the next two years the rent would be reduced from £1950 to £1700 and that he would be at liberty to leave the farm following that time.[166] This worked for a few years, but from November 1883 he began to accrue

159. DUSC GRE/X/P125/1.
160. DUSC GRE/X/P253.
161. DUSC GRE/X/P234.
162. DUSC GRE/X/P182.
163. DUSC GRE/X/P68.
164. DUSC GRE/X/P254.
165. DUSC GRE/X/P271.
166. DUSC GRE/X/P226.

arrears which he never paid off.[167] In 1884 he took a new lease of the property for three years that included a £200 allowance for lime and fodder.[168] From the expiration of this lease in 1887 he continued to fill in cultivation returns and may have been renting the property from year to year. It appears that his relationship with his landlord and the land agents was deteriorating, as a letter between two of the agents says that he had attempted to have most of the £200 allowance for linseed cake, when only £100 should have gone to this. Cleghorn, the author of the letter, describes Lumsden as a 'slippery character' and warns MacDonald, the recipient, to 'keep an eye on him'.[169] This evidence appears to show an interest on Lumsden's part in particular improvements, but from 1887, however, he took four successive crops of grain on Night Close and three on South Kirkhill and North Constable.[170] This would have exhausted the land and is contrary to the terms of all previous leases of Learmouth. It also suggests that he was more interested in extracting profit from the farm than in abstract notions of improvement and efficiency. By May 1888 Lumsden's arrears amounted to £1000, and a letter of 1 November implies that he had been asked to leave.[171] It was written by Albert Grey to George Grey and discusses a letter from Lumsden to Albert. Albert Grey appears to have disliked the tone of the letter and remarks that Lumsden should realise that he had been treated with 'indulgence'. He goes on to discuss the collection of the remaining arrears and the harvesting of the awaygoing crop.[172] The last cropping return for Learmouth was filled in by Mr Fox, Grey's steward, who had probably been farming East Learmouth on Grey's behalf since Smith surrendered his lease. This contains details for both 1889 and 1890, suggesting that Lumsden did not complete a return in his final year on the property. An annotation on the edge of the document notes that it would take several years to return the farm to its proper value following the irregular cropping.[173] An 1892 survey provides further evidence that William Piper Lumsden damaged the farm, although the surveyor noted that West Learmouth was in better condition than he expected.[174] In November 1888 Lumsden paid off his arrears with a cheque for £1500.[175] He commissioned a report by Messrs Turnbull and Calder giving a favourable view of his management of the farm,[176] which he used to claim compensation from Grey, and wrote to Grey on 11 March 1889 giving a detailed list of items for which

167. DUSC GRE/X/V25.
168. DUSC GRE/X/P221.
169. DUSC GRE/X/P286.
170. DUSC GRE/X/P271.
171. DUSC GRE/X/V25, DUSC GRE/X/P115/5.
172. DUSC GRE/X/P115/5.
173. DUSC GRE/X/P271.
174. DUSC GRE/X/P57.
175. DUSC GRE/X/V25.
176. DUSC GRE/X/P96.

he claimed compensation.[177] This included cattle cake from 1887 to 1889, bones, kinate and nitrate from 1884 to 1888, and damage done by the landlord by failing to drain and maintain the fences.[178] Again, this shows an interest in some areas of improved farming, though the extent may be exaggerated or the report entirely fabricated.

The cropping returns also show that several fields of West Learmouth were put down to permanent pasture from 1887 onward, including South-East Moor, South-West Moor, North-East Moor, North-West Moor, Piperdown and Middle Moor. This may show that the agricultural depression made it difficult for Grey to find a tenant, thereby requiring him to retain Lumsden on whatever terms he would accept. The need to reduce rent and increase the area of pasture may show that Lumsden was struggling to make a profit. Overall, it appears that Lumsden's farming was a mixture of the good – four- or five-course rotations selected with soils in mind, lime and artificial fodders – and the bad – taking successive crops of corn on certain fields and the reduction of some to permanent pasture. It appears that Lumsden used improved husbandry to increase output rather than in response to a sense of moral duty to use land efficiently.[179] He may, however, have done so from necessity, as he appears to have suffered from the effects of the late nineteenth-century agricultural depression.

In all, the data from Learmouth demonstrate that both the landlord and tenant had essential roles in improvement. Both probably acted from motives of profit and prestige, although at least in the case of William Piper Lumsden profit was more significant. This may, in turn, be due to the economic climate in which he farmed. Tenants and landlords also responded to developments in agricultural technology, as some of the improvements are associated with high farming.

At Learmouth, therefore, as in all our other townships, we have observed a wide range of improving methods. Across our five case studies these included both permanent changes to fixed capital, such as buildings and drainage, and temporary improvements, such as manuring and certain crop rotations. None of the improvements recorded are particularly unusual, although the frequency of river and stream improvement is greater than expected given the scholarly focus on under-draining.[180] Many of these introductions correspond to changes in technology; for example, much of the evidence for drainage at Howick dates from the mid-nineteenth century, after the invention of cheap extruded

177. DUSC GRE/X/P233.
178. DUSC GRE/X/P233.
179. Cf. Tarlow, *Improvement*, p. 35.
180. A.D.M. Philips, *The underdraining of farmland in England during the nineteenth century* (Cambridge, 1989); H. Cook and T. Williamson (eds), *Water management in the English landscape* (Edinburgh, 1999); P. Brassley, 'Land drainage', in J. Thirsk (ed.), *The agrarian history of England and Wales, volume VII 1850–1914* (Cambridge, 2000).

drainage pipes.[181] Similarly, many of the methods associated with high farming, particularly the introduction of oil-cake as a fodder and imported manures such as guano, appear to have been widely used, even by those farmers who did not take a full interest in improvement. Finally, the creation of farmsteads consisting of ranges of buildings around a yard, as at West Learmouth and almost all of the Longhorsley farms, is a result of increasing understanding of the importance of the preservation of manure.[182] It is too simple to say that new inventions were introduced as soon as they were discovered because of some obvious superiority, but technological development did have a role, albeit a limited one, in the introduction of improvements.

For an improvement to be introduced it was also necessary that farmers were aware of it. Consequently, it may be more important to study the way in which the knowledge of improvements spread. Unfortunately, there is only very limited evidence for this in the cases examined above. The cuttings taken from agricultural journals by Frederick Grey in the mid-nineteenth century and his investigation of the cattle-feeding methods of Lord Prudhoe are examples of two processes by which this may have happened. By improving, and through doing it in ways which were visible to his peers, Frederick Grey was participating in a fashionable activity. This itself appears to have been a reason to improve, although it is very difficult to identify confidently. The ornamentation on many of the cottages in the Howick estate village, does, however, suggest that they were not simply functional (Figure 6.1), and the establishment of the model farm at Howick Redstead was probably also motivated by fashion, as such farms were intended to be shown to visitors.

Fashion is often thought to be at odds with economic motivations for improvements, but this is not necessarily the case; fashionable improvements could increase profitability, especially as the fashion was to show an extensive knowledge of agriculture. Economic factors could be associated with the introduction of improvements in two ways. Firstly, increased profits could provide a motive for improvement and, secondly, capital was needed to introduce many husbandry methods. In both cases improvements would be linked to changes in the fortunes of the individuals involved, which in turn could be influenced by national economic trends. The phases of improvement at Howick both occur at times of agricultural prosperity, as well as being associated with the arrival of new owners. Similarly, much of the rebuilding at Learmouth occurred during the mid-nineteenth century, when prices for agricultural products were relatively high. The rebuilding at Bigge's Quarter in Longhorsley may also be associated with the rise in grain prices associated with the Napoleonic War. Indeed, this may have been Charles Bigge's motivation for buying the land. In all these cases the influence of economic factors could be in either motivating people to improve for

181. Brassley, 'Land drainage', p. 516.
182. Harvey, *History of farm buildings*, pp. 66–110.

profit or the provision of capital. One mechanism by which this capital reached farms was through the advance of capital by estates for improvements to buildings and drainage carried out by the tenants. In this way the estate or landlord made their mark in terms of improvements on particular tenanted farms. This has been seen many times, especially in the improvement of buildings and drainage at Learmouth and Howick Sea Houses, changes that were made at the same time as improvements to other Howick estate farms. The fact that these improvements were not made on all Howick estate farms, however, means that only some tenants took advantage of the provision of estate capital. This can be demonstrated by the instance in which Ralph Compton refused new piggeries on the grounds that he could not have paid the interest.[183]

None of these factors can be seen as a prime mover in the introduction of improvements. All seem to be equal and to interact with one another. So, for example, a particular tenant may have the capital to carry out improvements, the awareness of improved methods and the desire to improve for profit or status. These things themselves come from elsewhere; for example, the capital may be the result of estate policy or national economic trends, whereas awareness comes from reading agricultural journals or speaking to neighbours. We will consider the relationships between each of these influences in the following chapter.

183. DUSC GRE/X/P68.

7

Actors and mediation

Up to now we have explored the complexity of some of the principal processes at work in the post-medieval landscape without trying to reach any kind of explanation or understanding of them. As suggested above (Chapter 1), actor-network theory (ANT) may offer a way around some old problems with reaching such an understanding. It is hoped that ANT will allow us to come to terms with the complexity of the groups of people and things involved in any local occurrence of any of these processes. Our five themes – enclosure, farm consolidation, land-use redistribution, settlement dispersal and improvement – each involve different actors; in fact, every occurrence of each includes different combinations of actors. It is tempting to try to select one agent as the prime mover in each type of event, or to build a generalised model which attempts to explain all instances of enclosure, settlement dispersal and so on. These lines of reasoning would allow us to identify causes, something which is instinctively desirable. However, as described above (Chapter 1), non-representational theories usually reject generalising models and explanations because these cannot fully describe the mediation and assemblage of actors.[1] We will now attempt a different approach, examining carefully how particular actors were mediated and assembled. In Chapter 1 we examined the idea that events emerge from assemblages of actors, and that all actors are themselves assemblages of other actors. The description of these assemblages provides our approach to the events that we wish to understand. As we shall see, it is impossible to find a single way in which actors were assembled, or a single assemblage of actors, associated with any type of event. This means that generalising models and explanations are quite unable to come to terms with the complexity of local events. Some of the most obvious actors present in the five types of action will be described below. This list cannot be complete, but the mediation of each will be described. The importance of many of these actors has been recognised individually in previous studies; however, they have never been taken together and understood as an assemblage from which action emerges.

1.   Latour, *Reassembling the social*, p. 59.

People

One agency which comes across very clearly in our examples is that of individuals. Changes to the landscape often occurred immediately after a new person inherited or entered a particular farm, so such changes could be ascribed to that person. The idea that individuals were responsible for improvement and enclosure was a mainstay of traditional histories of the agricultural revolution. According to such approaches, a small number of individuals developed breeds, varieties, machines and techniques through experimentation, while others promoted these through publications. Typically, lists of such individuals include Jethro Tull, who is credited with advances in seed-drilling; Arthur Young, who wrote many agricultural books and was the first secretary of the Board of Agriculture; Robert Bakewell, who bred livestock; and Charles Townsend, who is associated with crop rotation, including the use of turnips. The discoveries made and publicised by these people were thought to be responsible for the national increase in agricultural output which comprises the agricultural revolution.[2] Such explanations are simplistic and have rightly been criticised, with some scholars scrutinising the importance of particular individuals. For instance, there were serious problems with the sheep and cattle breeds created by Bakewell, who also inherited an improved farm rather than being responsible for all improvements on his estate.[3] He was therefore more of a self-publicist than an innovator. More fundamentally, the agricultural books written by these experts were often criticised by smaller tenant farmers with practical experience.[4] The influence upon ordinary farming of the other major form of dissemination of agricultural ideas, the model farm, has also been criticised.[5]

The traditional model, therefore, appears to be flawed. However, our interest is local instances of landscape change, not national-scale trends in output, which were the focus of traditional accounts. At this scale individuals may have a role; for instance, the duke of Bedford appears to have been an important force for innovation on his own estates, principally through enclosure.[6] Similarly, the seventh earl of Carlisle was strongly involved with the improvement of his estate, as it became more acceptable for Whig politicians to be involved in agriculture

2. E.g. Prothero, *English farming*, pp. 148–206.
3. N. Russell, *Like engend'ring like: heredity and animal breeding in early modern England* (Cambridge, 1986), p. 146; D.L. Wykes, 'Robert Bakewell (1725–1795) of Dishley: farmer and livestock improver', *Agricultural History Review*, 52 (2004), p. 38.
4. H. Holmes, 'The circulation of Scottish agricultural books during the eighteenth century', *Agricultural History Review*, 54 (2006), pp. 61–8; S. MacDonald, 'The diffusion of knowledge among Northumberland farmers, 1780–1815', *Agricultural History Review*, 27 (1979), pp. 30–39.
5. S. Wade-Martins, *The English model farm: building the agricultural ideal, 1700–1914* (Oxford, 2002), p. 5; S. MacDonald, 'The model farm', in G.E. Mingay (ed.), *The Victorian countryside* (London, 1981), p. 224.
6. Brown, 'Reassessing the influence'.

from the mid-nineteenth century.[7] In addition, we have already seen that particular wealthy investors may have prompted the desertion of villages as they improved newly purchased estates.[8] Such activities may have created an atmosphere for improvement within a county; for example, Oxfordshire, which lacked a major improver, was less agriculturally advanced.[9]

Taken together, these examples show that the will of an individual landowner could be a powerful agency on their own farm or estate, though it is debatable whether this influence diffused beyond their direct control. Most published examples relate to members of the aristocracy precisely because of the large volume of documentation describing their actions. Similar examples, and some which highlight the agency of tenant farmers and small landowners, have been observed in our Northumberland townships.

Such agency has been demonstrated at Milfield, as Josephine Butler's suggestion that her father was responsible for the Milfield Common enclosure seems to be supported by the close correspondence between his arrival at Milfield Hill and the earliest evidence for the discussion of enclosure between the freeholders. Similarly, William Mills, George Grey's immediate predecessor at Milfield, seems to have been a keen engrosser and played an important role in the enclosure of Milfield's arable lands. William Mills is first recorded as a Milfield tenant in 1723 in a rental of the Howick estate.[10] In this document he was a joint tenant with Thomas Mills, but he became the sole tenant between the end of the rental in 1729 and the first surviving lease of the property of 1735. Prior to 1723 the property was let to John Pringle, John Cunningham and Thomas Nathaniel, so it is likely that Thomas and William Mills had engrossed the farm. In addition to Milfield Hill, William Mills also became a tenant of Milfield Demesne, from John Orde, and in partnership with George Burn, between 1741 and 1778.[11] This made William Mills at least joint tenant of nearly all the land in Milfield township. The enclosure of Milfield's arable in 1777 coincides closely with the renewal of William Mills' lease of Milfield Demesne and an apparent attempt at abolishing the tithes of Milfield by George Burn.[12] It appears that William Mills, like his successor, was important in ensuring that enclosure occurred.

Anthony Compton of Learmouth was also important in engrossing the leasehold farms to allow enclosure and settlement dispersal. He is first mentioned in connection with Learmouth in a 1708 rental, not as a tenant in that year but as

7. Gent, 'Seventh earl of Carlisle'.
8. Wrathmell, 'Deserted and shrunken villages'; Wrathmell, 'Village depopulation'; Dixon, 'Deserted villages of Northumberland'.
9. Brown, 'Reassessing the influence', p. 187.
10. NRO 1356/F/1.
11. NRO/1356/A/15.
12. NRO 1356/A/15.

the land agent.[13] He began to engross farms at Learmouth in 1719, while he lived in Berwick-upon-Tweed, where he was an alderman.[14] He continued to acquire leasehold farms until 1733, when he held the whole township.[15] The 1733 leases describe Compton as 'of Learmouth', suggesting that he had moved there after 1724, when he had been styled 'of Berwick'. It is likely that Compton built the farm at West Learmouth, as the earliest evidence for this is a plan of 1793, although the surviving building is early nineteenth century.[16] Compton's actions were also important in creating unity of control, which both formed a ring-fenced farm and allowed his successors to enclose easily. In the event this was done by his great-nephew Ralph Compton in 1799.

Many of the people described above were substantial gentry farmers, but the less wealthy also had a part to play. For instance, Thomas Pinkney engrossed farms at Longhorsley. In 1740 he took the lease of farms previously occupied by William Bell and William Grey[17] and had much work done on the farmhouse, as the rental records £2 8s 4d spent on the house itself and £3 13s 9d spent by the estate on building a milkhouse. This is higher than the amounts spent on other tenants.[18] He does not seem to have been successful, however, as he left in the following year.[19] Similarly, Robert Swann may have entered a newly created farm formed from some strips of land in the south of the township, as his rent is greater than that of his predecessor by £1. It is possible that this farm was created at his suggestion or at least through his negotiation. Like Pinkney, he had improvements made.

Robert Keith was another particularly active small tenant farmer. He rented Knightside and Spartishaw in Elsdon from William Orde in 1848.[20] He also took the lease of Townhead from Thomas Hall-Laidler on 25 September 1872, remaining the tenant of this property until the end of the nineteenth century.[21] On 21 July 1881 he added the Batt Field to his holding, but lost the lease of this in 1894 following a dispute with the landlord over the repair of buildings.[22] A letter of 31 March 1898 from Matthew Hall to James Cooper, who was managing The Batt and Townhead lands, remarks that Keith had recently become tenant of the Rothbury Charity lands, and describes this as 'another branch up the tree of life for Robert

13. DUSC GRE/X/P80.
14. DUSC GRE/X/P73.
15. DUSC GRE/X/P73.
16. DUSC GRE/X/P276; <http://list.english-heritage.org.uk/resultsingle.aspx?uid=1042197>, accessed 16 March 13.
17. CAS N/113.
18. CAS N/113.
19. CAS N/113.
20. NRO ZBS/14/1.
21. NRO ZBS/25/1.
22. NRO ZBS/25/1.

Keith'.[23] Keith was a particularly demanding tenant; he asked for a reduction of the Townhead rent in 1898, threatening to quit the farm if he failed to receive it.[24] He also took a disrespectful approach to the landlord, delaying his reply and writing that he expected that the reduction would be granted.[25] In addition, he asked for repairs to be made to a building on the Batt Field in 1887. The managers of the estate seem to have taken this badly as, had he asked for the repair before he took the lease, they could have had more rent.[26]

All these examples are tenants, but landlord or landowner agency is also important. One of the most obvious examples occurred at Howick, where the earliest important landowner, Edward Grey, bought up most of the land in the township between 1593 and 1623. He also made an agreement with John Craster to enclose a small piece of land which he was unable to purchase in 1607.[27] Finally, he appears to have been responsible for the enclosure of the remainder of the township, by unity of control, in the first half of the seventeenth century. From the beginning of the nineteenth century the activities of Howick's owners become more visible as documentary sources increase, and a pattern of change occurring immediately after the inheritance of the estate by each new generation emerges. The first instance was between 1804 and c.1830, beginning only three years after Charles, the second Earl Grey, moved into Howick Hall, his uncle Henry Grey having retired in 1801, and four years before his inheritance of the estate in 1808.[28] From around 1830 there is much less improvement on the Howick home farm, which probably coincides with Charles Grey's term as prime minister, which started in 1830.[29]

Activity began again in the 1840s following the inheritance of the estate by Henry, the third Earl Grey,[30] although, as most estate correspondence is signed by Frederick Grey, Henry's younger brother, the estate appears to have been managed by him. This period included the creation of a model farm at Redstead. Grey seems also to have taken an interest in agricultural literature, making cuttings from periodicals and corresponding with neighbouring farmers (see Chapter 6). This period ended around 1861, when Frederick Grey was appointed First Lord of the Admiralty, so improvement may have slowed as he acquired more political

23. NRO ZBS/25/1.
24. NRO ZBS/25/1.
25. NRO ZBS/25/1.
26. NRO ZBS/25/1.
27. DUSC GRE/X/P112.
28. Smith, *Lord Grey*, p. 136.
29. Smith, *Lord Grey*, p. 258.
30. Bateson, *Northumberland*, p. 352.

Figure 7.1 Linden Hall, the mansion built by Charles William Bigge at Longhorsley.

responsibility.[31] When Albert, fourth Earl Grey, inherited the estate in 1894 there was no new period of improvement, which may reflect a lack of interest on his part. There were, however, many changes to the way in which labour on the estate was managed, including the construction of a school and the introduction of profit-sharing and cow-keeping schemes (see Chapter 6). Changes at the Howick estate appear to correlate very well with the arrival of new landowners and thus clearly indicate the agency of particular individuals.

A similar phenomenon can be seen at Longhorsley in 1808, when the earl of Carlisle's estates at Bigge's Quarter were purchased by a man called Charles William Bigge.[32] One of his most obvious impacts on the landscape was the construction of a neo-classical mansion called Linden Hall and the laying out of a park around it (Figure 7.1). He also appears to have rearranged the farm boundaries to create larger farms with more regular shapes (Figure 7.2). The farmsteads depicted on a plan of 1773 are also very different from those depicted on the 1842 tithe plan, and, as there is little evidence in the Howard of Naworth papers for building work after 1773, it is likely that this rebuilding was carried out

31. A. Lambert, 'Grey, Sir Frederick William (1805–1878)', in *Oxford dictionary of national biography* (online edn, Oxford, 2004) <http://www.oxforddnb.com/view/article/50204>, accessed 1 July 2013.

32. CAS N/13/15.

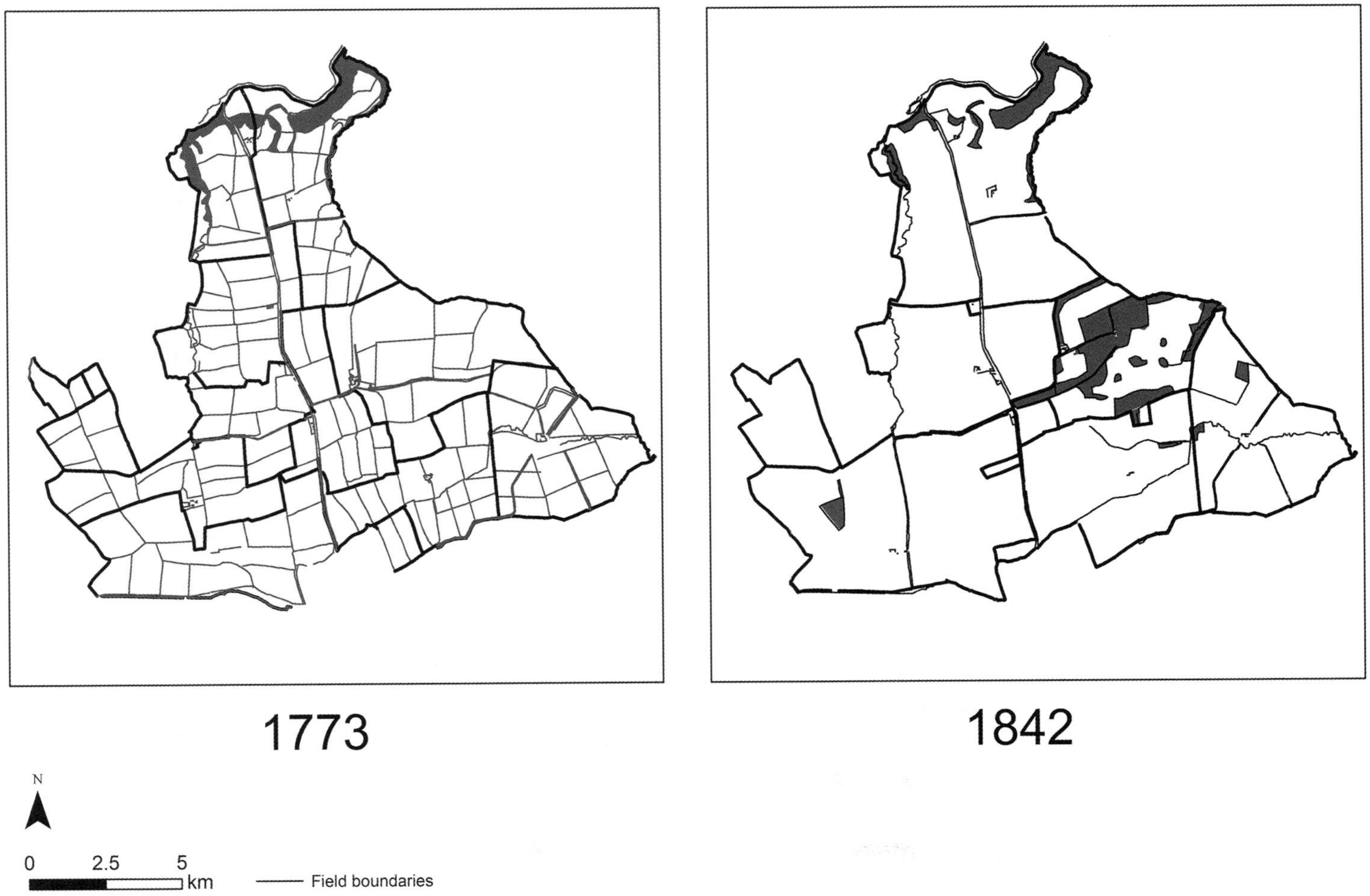
1773
1842
N
0
2.5
5
km
Field boundaries

Figure 7.2 Plans showing changes to farm boundaries in Bigge's Quarter between 1773 (DUSC N190/97) and 1842 (NRO DT43M). The farm boundaries have clearly been rationalised, probably at the same time as the creation of Linden Hall. The 1842 plan also shows the plantations forming the park around Linden Hall in the east of the township.

by Charles William Bigge (see Chapter 6). At the same time View Law was built on an entirely new site. As at Howick, a new owner seems to have ushered in a period of modernisation and improvement.

In contrast to those who were closely involved in improvement and enclosure, certain people took very little interest. The heirs of Thomas Pearson are a good example. Thomas Pearson built up an estate in Elsdon by purchases in 1766 and 1768.[33] This was divided between his sons, Francis and Thomas, at his death in 1775.[34] Francis Pearson was clearly planning to sell his estates in 1815, as he suffered a common recovery of them in that year.[35] He finally sold them to Thomas Thornton of Harwood in 1820.[36] Francis lived in Middlesex,[37] so it is possible that distance from the estates in Northumberland meant that he took little interest in them; he certainly must have had other sources of income. His brother Thomas died in 1817, leaving his share of the Elsdon estates to his son Thomas. This Thomas sold up shortly after, in 1825, again to Thomas Thornton.[38] As with Francis, neither the elder nor the younger Thomas lived at Elsdon; both lived in Newcastle, and both were master mariners.[39] In another example, James Ogle of Longhorsley seems to have opposed the 1664 enclosure agreement to such an extent that his lands had to be left out.[40] This meant that the enclosure was not completed until 1688, when Ogle's farm was purchased by Mr Bulman, who had supported the 1664 enclosure, and parts exchanged with Edward Horsley Widdrington.[41] This is not to say, however, that these people were without agency; their sales allowed people who did instigate landscape change to purchase their estates and caused them to purchase at particular times.

Other people did not make improvements despite continuing in possession of their estates. A good example is Aislabie Proctor. He was the incumbent of Alwinton, which had some glebe land in Elsdon. Proctor seems to have taken very little interest in this property and appears to have had only a very vague idea of what he possessed in Elsdon. For example, he claimed that he had not heard of a piece of land called 'Threep Land' mentioned in the lease of part of his estate called Bainshaw Bog.[42] Similarly, he had to write to a resident of Elsdon to ask where one of the gardens that he owned was and to whom he had let it.[43] In

33. NRO ZBS26/1.
34. NRO ZBS/26/2.
35. NRO ZBS/26/2.
36. NRO ZBS/26/2.
37. NRO ZBS/26/2.
38. NRO ZBS/26/2.
39. NRO ZBS/26/2.
40. NRO 358/21/10.
41. NRO 335/21/1.
42. NRO ZHE/14/3.
43. NRO ZHE/14/3.

addition, he did not sign the lease of Bainshaw Bog as, he notes, 'I suppose I ought to have done'.[44] He also let Cheek Gate from year to year and by word of mouth, a method which could be easily exploited.[45] This attitude may arise from the distance of the lands from his main holdings in Alwinton and his profession as a clergyman, rather than a landlord. He attempted to sell some of his land in 1874; however, despite the auction being held the sale fell through, as the land still appears in glebe terriers of 1895.[46] It is possible that the legal status of the land as glebe made the sale impossible. The agency of Aislabie Proctor made a difference to how the landscape developed, as his methods appear to have been exploited by tenants such as the Thorntons, who let the fences between Proctor's land and their own decay so that they could run stock across the whole area. Indeed, they may have rented some of these lands knowing that the way in which they were let could work to their advantage. This is a form of agency, albeit unintentional, as it shapes the way in which landscape change occurred.

Finally, there were some tenants who did not participate in improvement. Ralph Compton, for example, was the tenant of East Learmouth farm in the mid-nineteenth century, while one William Smith was the tenant of West Learmouth. There is evidence for building work at both farms up to 1846, but only at West Learmouth from 1846–7 (see Chapter 6).[47] It is probably significant that the building at East Learmouth stopped earlier, as an 1845 report relating to the farms stated that Compton had said that he needed more accommodation for pigs but did not want to pay the interest on the capital invested by the landlord.[48] In 1848 Compton became bankrupt and left the farm.[49] At the same time William Smith surrendered his lease of West Learmouth, which went in hand until 1851, when it was let to John Lumsden.[50] Building work at West Learmouth ceased on William Smith's departure, suggesting that he was the impetus behind it.[51] In the same year a man called William Smith, who may well be the former tenant of West Learmouth, took the lease of East Learmouth and immediately instigated a programme of building.[52] It seems, then, that building work ceased when tenants were unwilling to have it done. Their reasons for this may not always have been personal preference, as Ralph Compton's financial situation probably prevented him from taking on improvement.

44. NRO ZHE/14/3.
45. NRO ZHE/14/3.
46. NRO ZHE/14/3, NRO DN/E/9/1/103.
47. DUSC GRE/X/P182, DUSC GRE/X/P233, DUSC GRE/X/P233, GRE/X/P234.
48. DUSC GRE/X/P68.
49. DUSC GRE/X/P233.
50. DUSC GRE/X/P253.
51. DUSC GRE/X/P182, DUSC GRE/X/P233, DUSC GRE/X/P234.
52. DUSC GRE/X/P182, DUSC GRE/X/P233, DUSC GRE/X/P234.

Thus, our case studies show that people possessed agency in all types of landscape change considered here. This is problematic for studies which would draw simple correlations between events and economic or environmental trends.[53] If the relationship were a simple one, changes to tenants or landlords would make no difference to landscape development. It is also clear that all classes and social groups were involved in improvement and enclosure. Tenants, landlords, small owner-occupiers, gentry and aristocracy have all been shown to have been engaged in improvement. By the same token, some members of all these groups were ambivalent towards their estates or farms, and failed to take part in improvement or even disposed of their estates as soon as possible. In many cases their agencies are very similar. For example, Edward Grey, a member of the aristocracy, Anthony Compton, a wealthy tenant farmer, and Robert Keith, a much smaller tenant, all practised engrossment. They were also constrained by similar factors, such as the need to wait for a farm to pass to someone who was willing to sell it or give up a lease. As a result it is impossible to identify one group which caused improvement or enclosure. This is especially so because much of the agency is unintentional; many of the people who were uninterested in improvement nonetheless made a difference to the way in which it occurred within each township through neglect of their estates or their desire to dispose of them. Despite all this, correlations between economic trends and social groups do exist. I do not dispute the facts which such studies reveal; I simply show that, because individual effects come across clearly in local studies, such models are limited in their explanatory powers. Correlations occur because human agency emerges from an assemblage of different actors, some of which have been the subject of traditional models. These actors must now be considered.

Money

The importance of money in agricultural improvement has been discussed in economically deterministic scholarship. One of the most obvious suggestions made in such works is that the high grain prices of the Napoleonic Wars encouraged landowners to increase the area of arable cultivation through parliamentary enclosure.[54] Deterministic explanations have also been brought to bear on improvement, with the suggestion that investment slowed during the late nineteenth-century agricultural depression.[55] On the other hand, recent studies have begun to make more complex analyses of responses to price movements. For example, while many small farmers in Sussex were put out of business by the post-Napoleonic War depression, its effects were mediated by a number

53. Turner, *English parliamentary enclosure*.
54. Prince, 'Changing rural landscape', pp. 44–5; Turner, *English parliamentary enclosure*, p. 86; Chambers and Mingay, *Agricultural revolution*, p. 84.
55. Prothero, *English farming*, pp. 386–7.

of personal and local factors.[56] These include the poor rate burden, the stage in the family life cycle and the number of children. A good example is provided by a tenant farmer called William Paddison, who survived the depression through a combination of good decisions and a favourable situation.[57] Similarly, yearly price fluctuations during the late nineteenth-century depression were too great for individual farmers to have been able to perceive long-term trends in favour of livestock production clearly enough to be able to make decisions based on them.[58] Studies such as these begin to express how economic trends were mediated by local actors, including individuals. The importance of this is demonstrated by the five townships.

Many of the people who made the greatest changes were wealthy individuals. Anthony Compton, who engrossed the leasehold farms at Learmouth, was an alderman of Berwick,[59] and so was probably quite wealthy. This would have allowed him to stock a relatively large farm and made him a more attractive tenant for the landlord.[60] Consequently, his wealth was essential for him to make changes to the landscape. Similarly, Thomas Pearson had a non-landed income from a quarry which he owned at Walbottle, and left a large estate at his death.[61] He almost certainly invested money from this business in his purchases of land at Elsdon. Charles William Bigge, who bought and improved Bigge's Quarter in Longhorsley, was a Newcastle banker and died a wealthy man.[62] The example of Robert Keith, discussed above, provides the opposite case, as, while he practised engrossment, he did so on a scale which matched his smaller resources. Thus, access to capital was clearly important in being able to achieve landscape change or agricultural improvement.

Similarly, a lack of capital resources could cause an endeavour to fail. Many examples of this have been described elsewhere; for example, a scheme to drain East Flanders Moss in Perthshire failed because it was underfunded.[63] In general, it is likely that small farms were less able to compete, and that this was exacerbated by depressions or the high costs of parliamentary enclosure.[64] Some failures can also be found in our townships. A particularly clear example is that of Ralph Compton at East Learmouth, whose financial difficulties led him to refuse

56. Sheppard, 'Small farms'.
57. L. Crust, 'William Paddison: marsh farmer and survivor of the agricultural depression, 1873–96', *Agricultural History Review*, 43 (1995), pp. 193–204.
58. E.H. Hunt and S.J. Pam, 'Prices and structural response in English agriculture, 1873–1896', *The Economic History Review*, 50/3 (1997), pp. 477–505.
59. DUSC GRE/X/P73.
60. Mingay, 'The size of farms', pp. 473–4.
61. NRO ZBS/26/2.
62. DUSC DPRI/1/1850/B19/1–16.
63. Harrison, 'East Flanders Moss', pp. 9–10.
64. Mingay, 'The size of farms', pp. 471–2.

new piggeries offered by the landlord.[65] Similarly, James Wilson sold Milfield Demesne to John Orde in order to pay a debt. Wilson mortgaged the estate several times up to 1736, by which time it was encumbered with just over £1200.[66] He then assigned the lands to his son, who sold them to John Orde of Morpeth in 1741.[67]

It appears, then, that access to, or the lack of, capital was a major factor in determining the ability of an individual to cause landscape change. Personal fortunes could rise and fall as a result of purely local factors, but were more likely to be created in favourable economic conditions or to fall during depressions. Thus, personal wealth mediated national economic trends in local events. This can be seen quite plainly in some of the five townships, and is most clear at Howick South Side. This farm went in hand at the end of the 1810s, following a turbulent period of letting and reletting. Two tenants called Thompson left in 1814, and it was relet at the reduced rent of £1000 to a Mr William Jackson.[68] At this time a single field, South Whinney, and a cottage were detached from the main farm and let to a Mr Reavell.[69] William Jackson first experienced difficulty between October 1814 and March 1815, when he paid only £450 of his £500 half year's rent.[70] This was towards the end of the Napoleonic Wars and largely comprises the period of Napoleon's first exile. By October 1816 the arrears had reached £159 19s 0d, despite a reduction in the rent to £750 per annum.[71] Jackson had died by March 1818 and his executors paid off his debts in the following year.[72] After this South Side does not appear as a tenanted farm, suggesting that it had been taken in hand because other tenants could not be found. Similar problems were experienced at Howick at the end of the nineteenth century. Messrs Aitcheson left Sea Houses in 1866, having begun to accrue arrears in 1860. After this the farm was in hand until the end of the nineteenth century. The arrears accrued by the Aitchesons cannot be connected with the late nineteenth-century depression, as this did not begin until the 1870s; however, the fact that no new tenant was found probably is.

It is clear, then, that individual fortunes, which allowed improvement to be carried out, were partly determined by large-scale economic trends. Thus, in many cases economic downturns were a halt to improvement. However, depressions could offer certain opportunities, particularly to tenant farmers. This is revealed by a dispute between Ralph and Fenwick Compton (the tenants of Learmouth at the beginning of the nineteenth century) and their landlord, the second Earl Grey. In 1818, three years after the end of the Napoleonic Wars,

65. DUSC GRE/X/P68.
66. NRO ZBS/14/1.
67. NRO ZBS/14/1.
68. DUSC GRE/X/P81.
69. DUSC GRE/X/P81.
70. DUSC GRE/X/P81.
71. DUSC GRE/X/P81.
72. DUSC GRE/X/P81.

the Learmouth leases were due for renewal. The process of negotiation is first mentioned in a letter of 14 January 1818, which states that the land agent, Mr Anderson, had met with Mr Compton (which one is not specified) and made no agreement.[73] A later letter mentions that Fenwick Compton was unhappy with planned alterations to the farm boundaries.[74] The Comptons also thought the rents being asked by Anderson too high.[75] It is likely that the Comptons knew that they could make greater demands of their landlord since the economic conditions following the end of the Napoleonic Wars had made finding tenants more troublesome,[76] but it is also possible that they had been made more desperate by lower grain prices. On 15 May 1818 Anderson forwarded a letter from Ralph Compton to Earl Grey in which Ralph claimed that he could not take on Sunnilaws as well as West Learmouth owing to his state of health. In the covering letter Anderson described his negotiations with an alternative tenant, Mr Thompson, whom he recommended to Grey.[77] This prompted action from the Comptons, who wrote directly to Grey accusing Anderson of treating them unfairly, and also told Mr Thompson that the farms were not tithe free, a condition which would significantly reduce their value.[78] As a result Thompson refused the farm, and Anderson again offered it to the Comptons on the grounds that they were 'respectable and old Tenants'.[79] They refused this offer, and Anderson considered approaching Thompson for a second time before letting it by proposals, as he felt that this would damage Grey's reputation as a landlord and attract the wrong sort of tenant.[80] On 22 June Anderson wrote to Grey to inform him that he had agreed to let East Learmouth to Fenwick, but had not made an agreement with Ralph. Ralph must have left shortly after this, and the fact that he paid all his outstanding rent at Whitsuntide 1819 may provide a date.[81] Several letters between 31 July and 18 September detail legal proceedings taken by Grey against Ralph Compton, although it is unclear exactly why.[82] Similarly, William Piper Lumsden was given significant indulgences, such as a reduction of his rent in 1888, despite being unable to pay rent regularly. It

73. DUSC GRE/B2/7/145.
74. DUSC GRE/B2/7/152, DUSC GRE/B2/7/156.
75. DUSC GRE/B2/7/168.
76. On 30 January 1818 Anderson remarked that 'I do now experience considerably more altercation and trouble in letting of Farms, than when I first entered into your Lordships service' (DUSC GRE/B2/7/152). On 22 June 1818 he remarked that the letting of the estate 'had occasioned him many a restless night' (DUSC GRE/B2/7/174).
77. DSUC GRE/B2/7/164.
78. DUSC GRE/B2/7/168.
79. DUSC GRE/B2/7/170.
80. DUSC GRE/B2/7/170.
81. DUSC GRE/B2/7/184.
82. DUSC GRE/B2/7/210, DUSC GRE/B2/7/214, DUSC GRE/B2/7/216. An arbitration award shows that Grey was successful in this (DUSC GRE/X/P80).

is probable that Grey allowed this because of the shortage of suitable tenants during the late nineteenth-century depression.[83]

This suggests that money was important in landscape change, but that it did not work predictably, as assumed by economically deterministic models. At all times there were landowners and tenants who were successful and those who were unsuccessful. Their failure or otherwise was a combination of economics, their own responses and other factors. Consequently, economic trends were only transported to particular events by their providing people with more or less money, which could lead to varying consequences. Economics also influenced people's expectations of seeing a return from an investment. The idea that economic trends are mediated through personal finances and perceptions of economic change helps to explain the variety of experiences of economic boom and depression revealed in our townships. This unpredictability is due to the fact that many other actors are present in each event.

Estates

The estates are one such actor. An estate could affect individual farms in several different ways. Firstly, it could select tenants of a particular type; substantial tenants were often preferred, as they could be trusted to stock a large farm, would invest in improvements and were less likely to fall into arrears.[84] The desires and financial means of the landlord could also be mediated through the estate as estate policy. This might make it easier or harder for tenants to have improvements made. Sometimes absentee landlords are thought of as particularly neglectful, but this was not always the case.[85] Estate policy could also reflect national economic trends: some estates became cautious about investment during the depression, while others responded by investing more heavily.[86] A further layer of complexity is added by the fact that estates were often managed by an agent or steward. This agent collected rent and performed administration on the instruction of the landlord. This means that a further person could bring their own ideas and methods to a particular area.

This all suggests that estates could mediate the economic trends discussed above. A few examples of their agency can be demonstrated in our townships. One of the best is the enclosure of Learmouth. This occurred in 1799, and is revealed by an account showing expenditure on hedges in that year.[87] It also shows expenditure on hedges at other properties of the Howick estate, namely Presson, Downham, Sunnilaws and Wark. Wark was also subject to a parliamentary

83. DUSC GRE/X/P226.
84. Mingay, 'The size of farms', pp. 471–2.
85. Beckett, 'Debate over farm sizes'.
86. S. Farrant, 'The management of four estates in the Lower Ouse Valley, Sussex, and agricultural change, 1840–1920', *Southern History*, 1 (1979), pp. 155–70.
87. DUSC GRE/X/P181.

enclosure, which was supported in parliament by the second Earl Grey, who inherited the Howick estate nine years later.[88] This suggests that the enclosure of Learmouth was part of an estate policy to enclose the Tweedside area, of which all these farms were a part. However, this may not be simply an example of the estate forcing its policy on the tenantry. The enclosure also coincided with the coming of age of Fenwick Compton, the younger brother of Ralph Compton, who was tenant of Learmouth. During the enclosure the estate was divided in two, creating East and West Learmouth Farms. It is possible that Ralph requested the enclosure to divide the farm to provide for his younger brother.[89] He would have been in a position to do this as Learmouth is by far the largest of the Tweedside farms, making him an important tenant. Thus, the estate not only mediated the agency of the landlord, but also that of the body of tenants as a whole, and of individual tenants, where they were of sufficient importance. Indeed, some firms of agents saw the representation of tenants as an important part of their duty.[90]

Another way in which the estate had agency in landscape change was in the provision of capital for buildings and drainage. During the later nineteenth century the Howick estate spent large amounts of money on many of its leasehold farms, as recorded in the 'Buildings' and 'Draining' Books.[91] Some was provided by government loans, through the Lands Improvement Company, most of which was spent on draining.[92] This money was not spent equally on all farms; in fact, some received none at all. It appears that it was spent only where tenants were able to pay interest on the investment so as to ensure a return for the estate.[93] Estate funds were also spent at the request of tenants, when they asked for a particular improvement.

It appears, then, that an estate's agency was not simply a case of the desires of the landowner being forced upon the tenantry. It was, instead, a combination of landlord and tenant interests. It also mediated national scale agencies. For example, drainage loans used in the second half of the nineteenth century were made available to compensate for the repeal of the Corn Laws.[94] Thus, the estate may be seen as a hybrid of several different actors; that is, they no longer appear as indivisible bounded entities because the boundary of the estate's agency is penetrated by fashions, knowledge and wealth from outside.[95]

88. *Journal of the House of Commons* (37 Geo III 22 May), 53, p. 594. Grey appears to have been part of the committee which examined the Bill.
89. DUSC GRE/X/P29.
90. B. English, 'Patterns of estate management in East Yorkshire, c.1840–c.1880', *Agricultural History Review*, 32 (1984), p. 42.
91. DUSC GRE/X/V101, DUSC GRE/X/V102–3.
92. DUSC GRE/X/P343.
93. See Philips, *Underdraining*.
94. D.C. Moore, 'The Corn Laws and high farming', *Economic History Review*, 18 (1965), pp. 554–5.
95. J. Wylie, *Landscape* (London, 2007), pp. 200–201.

Fashions

Another apparently external factor implicated in landscape change is fashion. This is occasionally cited as an explanatory factor by landscape historians. For instance, newly developed notions of privacy led tenants to live outside villages, resulting in settlement dispersal.[96] It is even more widely used by post-processual archaeologists, who have found that improvement was often a response to a sense of moral and patriotic duty. Contemporaries saw the agricultural production base as a prerequisite for, and index of, progress.[97] As a result, 'improvement' came to be valued irrationally.

A few examples from our townships demonstrate the importance of fashion. One of the clearest cases is the creation of the model farm at Howick Redstead by Frederick Grey. This farm may be compared with Pasture House, which is also part of the Howick demesne, but which was run for a profit. Redstead is much larger and contained many more specialist buildings and pieces of equipment than did Pasture House.[98] While all of the tools at Redstead are theoretically useful, some, such as the portable railway, were probably superfluous. Similarly, it was probably unnecessary to have several different types of plough. This suggests that the farm was being used for display more than for practical agriculture. Certainly, Grey was keen to share the results of his experiments at Redstead, as he answered a questionnaire on cattle farming in great detail, providing much information on the regime and his opinions on feeding boxes.[99] The fashion for agricultural improvement was, however, only brought to Howick by Grey as change began when he arrived. He was clearly particularly interested in agriculture, choosing to run the estate despite not being the legal owner (his elder brother was the actual heir). He also read many periodicals on agriculture, cuttings from which were sent to the estate office. In addition, he had his stewards ask other farmers in the area about their preferred methods of cattle feeding (see Chapter 6).[100] By these mechanisms Frederick Grey learnt both the techniques and doctrines of improvement.

By examining local detail it is possible to reach a more satisfactory understanding of these mechanisms, rather than attributing them to a vaguely defined 'society'. In each case examined here fashions were brought to a specific site or event by people who had read certain publications or had particular conversations. They also needed the financial means to pursue fashionable ideas. In short, as with economic forces, fashion was mediated locally by people and things. This means that some purely local factors can have a significant influence on local events.

96. Williamson, *Transformation*, p. 47.
97. Tarlow, *Improvement*, p. 35.
98. DUSC GRE/X/P254, DUSC GRE/X/P236.
99. DUSC GRE/X/P186.
100. DUSC GRE/X/P125/10.

Family relationships

Family relationships are a good example. Perhaps most obviously, strict settlement of estates upon heirs reduced the ability of landlords to raise capital for improvement until the law regarding this was reformed in the mid-nineteenth century.[101] Encumbrances also reduced estates' abilities to invest in improvement during the late nineteenth-century depression.[102] Conversely, newly wealthy individuals purchased land in order to provide an inheritance for their children.[103] Many examples of this can be seen in our townships. The clearest is that of William Dobson, who engrossed three leasehold farms at Longhorsley in 1677. He died shortly after, in 1699, and split them between his children: James, John and George.[104] Similarly, Thomas Pearson, who built a modest estate at Elsdon from 1766 to 1768, left it to his children, Thomas and Francis, in 1775, only ten years after he had begun to acquire it.[105] In a further example, two Thornton wills divided estates at Elsdon in 1814 and 1848; after the first will, Thomas Thornton, the eldest son, went about reconstructing the estate by purchase.[106] It was suggested above that Learmouth Farm was divided in two at enclosure in order to provide for a younger brother of the tenant, demonstrating a particularly distinctive way in which family relationships could divide estates. The close coincidence between Fenwick's coming of age and the date of the enclosure implies that Ralph Compton, who was tenant of Learmouth and brother of Fenwick, had suggested that the farm should be enclosed in order to supply an opportunity to divide the farm in two to provide for his brother. Family relationships were, therefore, a reason to create and divide estates.

They could also have quite unexpected consequences. The brothers Fenwick and Ralph Compton seem to have competed with each other during a rearrangement of boundaries at Learmouth. In fact, Ralph Compton remarked to the land agent that he made a high offer of rent 'in a passion for the sole purpose of defeating his Brother [sic.] of Clover Field and Kiln Close'.[107] Similar rivalry may be seen among the Thornton brothers at Elsdon. Thomas Thornton purchased several farms between 1810 and 1825;[108] the first was Scotch Arms, which was bought jointly with his father, Robert, on 12 May 1810.[109] Robert and

101. B. English, *The great landowners of East Yorkshire* (London, 1990), p. 89.

102. R.J. Colyer, 'Some aspects of land occupation in nineteenth-century Cardiganshire', *Transactions of the Honourable Society of Cymmrodorion* (1981), p. 92.

103. F.M.L. Thompson, 'Life after death: how successful nineteenth-century businessmen disposed of their fortunes', *Economic History Review*, 43 (1990), p. 44.

104. CAS N/12/10–11, CAS N/111.

105. NRO ZBS26/1–2.

106. NRO ZBS26/1–2.

107. DUSC GRE/B2/7/168.

108. E.g. NRO ZBS/26/2.

109. NRO ZBS/26/2.

Thomas also owned Mill Lands in partnership, so this was probably acquired under a similar arrangement.[110] His father's will of 1814 left a moiety of Mill Lands to Thomas' brothers Robert and Henry,[111] but it seems that this was interpreted by Robert and Henry as including Scotch Arms. Thomas seems to have disputed this, but eventually came to an arrangement with Henry to purchase his share in 1832. The other quarter remained with Robert Thornton the younger and passed to his son.[112] Another unexpected way in which family could influence the building of estates was exemplified by the attempt by Ralph Carr to join with his brother so that he would have enough money to purchase Bigge's Quarter, although in the event this did not occur.[113] It is likely that family connections led Edward Grey to establish his seat at Howick, as Greys had held land there since 1319, though their exact relationship with Edward is obscure.[114] It was also probably significant that the first purchase was from his brothers, Rodger and Arthur, who may have offered him a favourable price because of their relationship.[115]

Marriages, too, were often important. At Elsdon, Low and High Mote Farms were joined by marriage. The first indication of this is a deed poll of 1729, which devised the land to Elizabeth Hall and Matthew Hall for life and then to Elizabeth's daughter by her first marriage, Catherine, and her husband Jeremiah Bayles. This altered the outcome of the will of Elizabeth's first husband Robert Elsdon, who must have left it to her while she remained his widow.[116] It is likely that Matthew Hall owned Low Mote, as it was certainly the property of his son Alexander,[117] and other occupiers had often been Halls.[118] This may have caused the enclosure commissioners to place the allotments for the two properties together.

Family relationships appear to influence the creation and use of estates in many unexpected ways in addition to their traditional roles. For example, the idea that people built up estates in order to create an inheritance for their children is unsurprising and has been suggested in other studies; on the other hand, rivalry between brothers has rarely been thought of as an agent of landscape change. These are very personal, local factors, and yet appear to be as significant in local events as global factors such as prices and fashions. So, we could argue that Fenwick Compton's coming of age was just as important as the rising price of grain in causing enclosure at Learmouth, or at least in causing it to occur in 1799. The former, personal reason, is instinctively surprising for historians and

110. NRO ZBS/26/1.
111. NRO ZBS/26/1.
112. NRO ZBS/26/2.
113. NRO ZCE/F/1/1/1/209.
114. Bateson, Northumberland, p. 349.
115. DUSC GRE/X/P43.
116. NRO ZBS/26/2.
117. NRO ZBS/26/2.
118. Elsdon Parish Register, pp. 114, 141, 143, 164, 168, 171, 217, 221, 235.

social scientists, while the latter, economic explanation, seems common sense. However, the statement is true, the only difference being that Fenwick Compton's age could have no effect outside Learmouth, while grain prices could. In other words, grain prices are better connected and therefore global, while Compton's age is not. This is an important difference for explaining trends in the frequency of enclosure, but is unimportant in trying to explain enclosure specifically at Learmouth. When we realise that similar local factors must have operated in every landscape change it becomes clear that correlations between any global factor and landscape change are always incomplete explanations and that such models are necessarily blunt instruments.

Land, soil and climate

Environmental factors have often been invoked to explain landscape change. For instance, it has been argued that increasing regional specialism caused the agricultural revolution, relying heavily on the environmental conditions of different parts of the country to explain the form taken by landscape and agricultural changes.[119]

Some other examples may be observed in our townships. Firstly, many of the differences between the coastal and central plain townships, Howick and Longhorsley, and the other three are probably due to the environmental differences between them. Howick and Longhorsley had a greater proportion of arable than the other townships, and were also enclosed earlier. It is likely that the higher fertility of the soils in these townships made arable farming more profitable in them.[120] Thus, the fact that these were more favourable areas for cereal cultivation than the uplands has played an important role in the development of their landscape.

Environmental conditions also played a role in the development of local landscapes. A clear example is the distribution of post-enclosure ridge and furrow at Longhorsley. This correlates with neither farm nor estate boundaries and, therefore, cannot be *explained* by human agency. Unfortunately, it is not clear whether the distribution represents the extent of post-enclosure arable, the extent of ridge and furrow use or the extent of later cultivation which destroyed the ridge and furrow. Whatever the case, it is important to remember that although the location of the ridge and furrow reflects environmental conditions it is still a product of human action and inaction. We must assume, therefore, that all people at Longhorsley were equally aware of the potential of the land and the technologies available for cultivating it in ridges. Only this would lead them to act in similar ways and produce a pattern which appears to contain no human agency.

Pieces of waste left uncultivated after enclosure also provide examples of the influence of the environment on local landscapes. These include the common at

119. Williamson, *Transformation*.
120. Bailey and Culley, *General view*, pp. 2–3.

Longhorsley, which was reserved by the 1664 enclosure agreement. It was placed on the worst land in the area according to the Agricultural Land Classification.[121] Another piece of rough grazing near Cold Wells Field was left unimproved following the enclosure of Longhorsley, although it was technically enclosed. Finally, at Howick another piece of rough grazing called Harrow Hill and West, Middle and East Moor Fields was left uncultivated. In both cases the land in question was too wet to use. The enclosed pastures at Longhorsley and Howick were later drained, showing that, as technology reduced the cost of draining, the effect of environmental conditions changed. It is also important to realise that all these occurrences were a result of human decisions, as people had to understand or learn that land was uncultivable with the available technology or at a reasonable expense. The effect of human agency is especially clear at Howick. Here Harrow Hill was drained either during an early nineteenth-century phase, immediately after inheritance by the second Earl Grey, or during the mid-nineteenth century under his sons. Thus, the enthusiasm of certain people could also overcome environmental conditions. To point out human, monetary and technological agency in these events does not reduce the agency of the environment; it simply finds other agencies at work within it.[122]

Soils could also affect the way in which land reverted to waste during times of low grain prices. For example, much of the land at Elsdon and Learmouth, which went down to grass during the nineteenth century, was former common, and thus of poor quality. The fact that such pieces of land were chosen time and again as pasture is the result of environmental conditions. Finally, the environment affected the location of settlements. At Howick the late eighteenth-century model village was placed on a piece of former waste. This was because the site was chosen by Henry Grey, the owner of Howick, and not the people living in the village, who had to put up with damp cottages throughout the nineteenth century.[123] Similarly, Tithe Hill Farm was put on a piece of low-quality land. This farm was created by an agreement between Henry Grey, the landlord, and Ralph Compton, the tenant of Learmouth, to abolish glebe and certain tithes.[124] In this agreement Tithe Hill was granted to Compton in lieu of a moiety of the tithes of corn and grain and of the glebe. The difference in status between the two individuals may have allowed Grey to dictate where the farm was to go, and thus retain possession of the best land in the township. However, it is also likely that, as Compton would occupy all the land either as tenant or owner, he did not care which pieces he owned and which he rented.

---

121. Agricultural Land Classification <http://magic.defra.gov.uk/datadoc/metadata.asp?dataset=2>, accessed 15 August 2012; NRO 358/21/10.
122. Law, 'And if the global were small and non-coherent'.
123. DUSC GRE/X/P222.
124. DUSC GRE/X/P276.

Consequently, the ability of human actions to have an effect is mediated by the environment, while human actions can also form a part of the environment's effect.[125] The environment also created the need for agricultural changes, as particular landscapes were suitable for some practices and not others. Finally, it allowed some farmers to succeed and others to fail, as farms in favourable areas may have been better able to survive difficult economic circumstances.

Thus, like all our actors, soil and climate cannot be separated from their relationships with all other actors. It is not possible to separate out any of the agencies discussed above or to claim that an event was caused by any *one* factor. Each emerged from an assemblage. For example, the Learmouth enclosure involved the agency of Anthony Compton. However, his agency emerged from his wealth and desire to emulate the aristocracy. It also involved his successors, who actually carried out the enclosure. Ralph probably asked for the enclosure from the land agents. He possibly thought of the likelihood of a return from rising grain prices during the Napoleonic Wars, which may have provided him with money to defray the costs. The landscape itself also had agency. It was a suitable farm to enclose, as it was rich turnip land.[126] This attracted Compton to it, although the presence of glebe land probably prevented Compton from enclosing it himself. The relationship between Ralph and his brother Fenwick is also important, as Ralph may have wanted the enclosure in order to provide a farm for his brother. The estate also had some agency, as enclosure was part of a wider estate policy and because the estate provided capital which made it possible. There were also many other agencies which have not been described above. For example, the written leases and the laws on which they are based allow the engrossment, carried out by Compton, to survive and to allow his descendants to enclose. The list is not, and cannot be, complete: the examples discussed in this chapter are simply the most obvious and well documented. These actors were never assembled in the same way twice, and as such the similarities between different instances of one type of event, such as enclosure, are only ever superficial.

Some of these actors are, of course, non-human. This is not to suggest that non-human objects have intentions but that intention is not important; agency is just the ability to make a difference to an event. As human intentionality is examined it becomes clear that it emerges from an assemblage of actors. These include ideas, which have been picked up from reading and conversations, and the possibilities allowed by wealth and landscape.

It can be said that actors such as these are mediated by people, which raises an important point about the relationship between local and global. It has been shown that apparently global actors, such as economic trends, were made present

125. S. Harrison, S. Pile and N. Thrift (eds), *Patterned ground: entanglements of nature and culture* (London, 2004), pp. 9–10; Wylie, *Landscape*, pp. 200–201.
126. Bailey and Culley, *General view*, pp. 2–3.

in events only by local mediators, in this case people who were either wealthy or not, and who chose to spend their money in particular ways. This means that local factors are no less important than global factors, which are only ever present when made so by local mediators. As a result, studies of landscape change must allow for the agency of some unexpected actors, such as sibling rivalries, rather than cherry-picking 'acceptable' agents, as only then can they come to terms with the complexity of an event.

8

Conclusions

Throughout this book we have charted the transformation of five landscapes. The changes made at each place must have altered these five landscapes, and even the communities living in them, almost beyond recognition. Nonetheless, the five types of change explored here were incremental, not revolutionary. None appears to have happened in a single event in any one place, but usually as a series of events each concerning only a small area of land. This is perhaps an important way of understanding landscape formation: as, on the whole, the product of incremental change rather than of dramatic replanning. We can see the landscape as a constantly changing entity to which changes accrete over time, forming 'events' such as enclosure. The experience of this in any one landscape may have been a series of apparently insubstantial transformations, inconsequential by any particular individual. While we have been able to generalise to the extent of identifying trends, such as that towards dispersed settlement patterns, we have been unable to identify a common set of processes behind any one instance of these. Certainly, it has been shown that many alterations of the landscape often attributed to enclosure actually occurred as long processes usually operating on either side of enclosure itself. For instance, the consolidation of farms at Longhorsley occurred both before formal enclosure, through a process of piecemeal enclosure, and after, through the engrossement of leasehold property by tenants. Even enclosure behaves like this to some extent, as townships often experienced several enclosure events that were usually linked to processes of engrossment. The complexity of each process is striking, and it has proved impossible to identify one set of circumstances under which all instances of a given type of landscape change took place. It has been suggested that the complexity arises from the unique combination of actors which brought about the events in each case.

Actors and agency

Humans are among the most obvious actors in many of the events discussed. People from many different classes clearly made a great difference to how and when agricultural improvement and landscape change took place. The most obvious example is Howick, where the inheritance of the estate by each new generation ushered in a new era of improvement, while other commitments often prevented owners from continuing improvement. Tenants were equally if not more important. The most prominent example is Anthony Compton's engrossment of the leasehold farms at Learmouth. He was a particularly wealthy tenant, but the less wealthy, such as Robert Keith of Elsdon, were also ambitious and engrossed property in similar ways. Consequently, it is difficult to identify one social group which is particularly important in causing landscape change in the period. It is also important to realise that human agency is not restricted to the situations in which people were intentionally active or successful, as failure or inaction can make just as much difference to an event. A clear example of this is the failure of Thomas Pinkney's venture at Longhorsley, which provided an opportunity for the division of his farm. Similarly, the arrival of the fourth Earl Grey, who was much less interested in agriculture than his predecessors, ended the period of improvement at Howick. Thus, inaction and failure can also be an important form of agency. Uninterested landowners and tenants also came from all social backgrounds: at Longhorsley several small tenants made little improvement to their farm buildings, while at the other end of the social scale the fourth Earl Grey, as noted, made few changes to husbandry at Howick.

The desire and ability to develop the landscape, or alternatively to ignore it, emerge from an assemblage of other actors, which become visible through an examination of the people themselves. So, for instance, a person may act in a particular way because of the influence of fashion, economics or politics, which allow types of event to have trends at a national level despite the importance of local agency. This may best be understood through the late nineteenth-century agricultural depression, which clearly affected several of our case studies. For instance, William Piper Lumsden failed to farm successfully after 1873, improvement at Howick began to slow from the mid-nineteenth century and much of the reversion to waste which occurred at Elsdon happened probably at this time. None of these effects are the same. William Piper Lumsden was a tenant and so suffered difficulty through falling into arrears. Howick was farmed directly, so the Greys simply cut back on improvements. The changes at Elsdon are probably a reflection of both types of response, and perhaps a realisation that meat production was a better option than grain under late nineteenth-century conditions. The differences between them arise because the drop in the prices of agricultural products which constituted the depression was being mediated locally by different actors in each case. It is also important to realise that some tenants and landlords did not suffer during the agricultural depression, so it had an effect only where it impacted the personal finances of the farmers and landlords involved. Having understood this, we may detect the influence of economics in other cases. The rise in prices during the Napoleonic Wars may have been significant in prompting improvement at Howick and the enclosure of the Tweedside area of that estate, of which Learmouth is a part. The fall in prices after the war caused some Howick tenants to fall into arrears, while the tenants of Learmouth were emboldened by the lack of competition for their farm to demand lower rents. Finally, it is important to note that the bankruptcy of Ralph Compton of East Learmouth, which temporarily halted building work at his farm, was not the result of a wider economic downturn. This reinforces the idea that personal finances are of primary importance and form the channel through which national trends are mediated.

Economics are not the only global factor to be mediated locally; fashions were also important. The construction of landscape parks and neo-classical country houses at both Howick and Longhorsley are probably examples of the influence of fashion on the landscape. It is, however, clearest at Howick, where Frederick Grey adopted ideas from fashionable publications and was keen to demonstrate his knowledge through both correspondence and inviting visitors to his model farm.[1] Similarly, the fourth Earl Grey was influenced by changes in politics as social concerns became more important during the transition from Whigism to Liberalism.[2] This led him to concentrate his efforts more on the welfare of his labourers than on husbandry practice. As before, these fashions are present in the local interactions only where they are mediated by specific actors, in this case particular people. For example, Frederick Grey mediated knowledge which he acquired from books and conversations. From these he also gained an expectation that he would receive prestige by demonstrating knowledge. Thus, fashion is not unproblematically present in local conditions; it is brought there by particular people, and indeed publications and other media. As discussed above, other people were clearly less interested in mediating such ideas, or had less access to them. So we can now discuss traditional actors, such as economic trends, in the same terms as we discuss the actors of more recent theories such as fashions and worldviews.

Having reduced these two global factors to their local mediation, it is possible to understand purely local or personal factors on the same terms.[3] Each estate, as an institution, is an important local actor in many landscape changes, as each may have encouraged improvement or provided capital. The Howick estate was important in the enclosure of Learmouth, as this was clearly an estate policy undertaken at several neighbouring properties. On the other hand, it has been shown above that this enclosure was probably requested by Ralph Compton, tenant of Learmouth, in order to create a farm for his brother. It appears, then, that Ralph Compton requested enclosure which was then adopted as estate policy.

1.   DUSC GRE/X/P125/10, DUSC GRE/X/P186.
2.   Searl, *Liberal Party*, pp. 16–28.
3.   Latour, *Reassembling the social*, pp. 173–218.

It was probably adopted generally because Charles, second Earl Grey, was keen to improve his newly inherited estate, and because grain prices were high, thereby allowing a high return on his capital. Thus, an estate could mediate the agencies of both landlords and tenants, but was also an important part of the tenant's ability to create change, as permission and capital were both required. Similarly, the estate's desire to improve could be thwarted by unwilling tenants. This is clearly demonstrated by Ralph Compton's refusal of new piggeries in 1845.[4] As with all other actors, the agency of each estate is key to how events took place but is entirely different each time because of the other actors with which it is assembled. Such actors include the land, soil and climate. These could provide opportunities to pursue improved agriculture or could prevent it. It is notable that Learmouth and Milfield are among the most improved townships, as they have soils which are amenable to turnip agriculture. This was fashionable in the late eighteenth and early nineteenth centuries, so these townships attracted wealthy improvers such as George Grey and Anthony Compton. Soil and climate probably also caused some regional patterns, especially the early enclosure of Howick and Longhorsley, on the coast and central plain, and their high proportions of arable immediately before enclosure. Some environmental conditions shaped the nature of improvement locally, determining which fields would be improved or left as rough pasture. In addition, antecedent landscapes could either be a barrier or an opportunity. Those townships with the most fragmented patterns of landholding were often more difficult to enclose and consolidate, which made them unattractive to improvers. Consequently, tenure and environmental conditions were an important part of a person's ability to carry out landscape change. However, they also influenced which people were present in a particular area, as certain conditions were attractive to improvers. On the other hand, it was possible for someone with enough enthusiasm and money to overcome such difficulties; Charles William Bigge and the Boltons were thus able to create a ring-fenced holding at Blackpool Farm in Freeholder's Quarter where other landowners failed. These factors were mediated locally by the wealth and enthusiasm of particular people. As such, the environment is as much subject to human agency as vice versa. These local actors remind us that while 'global' actors such as fashion were important in creating enthusiasm for improvement, local factors were equally significant agents.

Thus, many different actors can be identified in each type of landscape change. However, each acts in a unique way in every event. This is because they act only within an assemblage of other actors. In short, actors behave in the way that they do only because of their relationships with other actors. Actor-network theory uses a behavioural ontology, meaning that actors exist only through acting, and so implies that actors exist only through their relationships with other actors.[5] These

---

4.   DUSC GRE/X/P68.
5.   A. Mol, *The body multiple: ontology in medical practice* (Durham, NC, 2002), pp. vii–viii, 6.

ideas require us to understand the past in a very different way. It is argued here that actor-network theory may be used to discuss individuals without privileging human intentionality, and non-humans without being determinist.

Using non-representational theory in history and archaeology

A number of important points have been made above. Firstly, global actors are global only because they are mediated in many different local events and by local actors; for instance, national prosperity is brought to a local interaction by personal wealth, while knowledge of fashions comes from personal reading and conversation. This means that local actors are as important as global ones in any particular event. This creates a large and complex assemblage of actors, making each event unique. As a result, rather than being unified phenomena, enclosure, consolidation, improvement, land-use change and settlement dispersal are all composed of series of unique events. They are only united in discussions by contemporaries or by modern historians and archaeologists. In each of these events every actor behaves in a unique way because of its relationship to the other actors involved. This means that it is not possible to build generalised models because the role of each actor is different in every case. Consequently, it is impossible to reach a satisfactory explanation of any type of event. It is, however, possible to describe thoroughly the actors involved in a particular local event, as has been done here. Latour in fact rejects the idea of explanation completely.[6] He suggests that either the assemblage of actors is fully described and an explanation superfluous, or that an explanation would just be another actor, and so adding it would only extend the description. Such a description has been given above of the various types of event at each township. It is, however, difficult to justify an approach that can only explain local instances of a phenomenon even if it is accepted that the phenomenon is a creation of archaeologists and historians more than an objective aspect of the past.

As has been suggested above, some actors are 'global' in that they are connected to more local events than other actors. Their identification is possible and may be used to suggest why types of landscape change were more common in particular periods than others. It must be acknowledged, however, that this does not explain the type of event fully. We have encountered such activities in the idea that the incidence of parliamentary enclosure was linked to the price of grain, or that improvement was related to settment dispersal.[7] In these cases the actors identified give insight into the timing of particular trends in landscape development. Similar arguments are used with non-traditional actors in studies which connect enclosure to the rise of individualism or to doctrines of

6.   Latour, *Reassembling the social*, p. 137.
7.   Turner, *English parliamentary enclosure*, pp. 106–34.

improvement.[8] This approach is valuable because it may show why enclosure, for instance, was more common in certain periods. It is, however, a very long way from explaining the causation of a type of event, as it does not describe the ways in which these agencies are mediated. By understanding global actors as things which are mediated locally we reach a better explanation of the anomalies which inevitably emerge in any attempt to correlate a cause and an event. Such 'noise' is usually dismissed; however, it may be more satisfactory to realise that it represents cases of mediation varying. Actor-network theory is not a solution on its own, but does provide both a different way to deal with the relationship between the local and the global and a starting point from which to address problems that were not accessible to determinist and post-processual theory. The understanding of mediation is especially important for local history, as it allows the connection between local causation and larger-scale models to be made rigorously.

Consequently, actor-network theory provides an important critique of the explanations offered by both traditional and post-processualist explanations of landscape change in the post-medieval period. It does not, however, offer an alternative explanation. Instead, it rejects the possibility of explanation in favour of description. This type of description has been attempted here and has revealed that there is a great disparity between current models of post-medieval landscape development and local events. This is because each landscape change emerged from a large variety of actors, of which 'global' actors, favoured in previous models, were only one type. At face value this is unsatisfying, as it denies the possibility of explaining landscape change. It does, however, draw attention to the way in which actors become global through building connections between different local events. We are thus presented less with a model for emulation and more with a different way of thinking about landscape processes which provides a starting point for moving away from deterministic explanations towards a more subtle form of understanding.

8.   Johnson, *Archaeology of capitalism*; Tarlow, *Improvement*.

Bibliography

Addy, J., *The agrarian revolution* (London, 1972).

Allen, R.C., *Enclosure and the yeoman: the agricultural development of the south midlands* (Oxford, 1992).

Ashton, T.S., *An economic history of England: the eighteenth century* (London, 1955).

Bailey, J. and Culley, G., *A general view of the agriculture of the county of Northumberland* (1797; 2nd edn, London, 1813).

Bateson, E., *A history of Northumberland*, Vol. II (Newcastle, 1895).

Beckett, J.V., 'The debate over farm sizes in eighteenth- and nineteenth-century England', *Agricultural History*, 57 (1983), pp. 308–25.

Beresford, M., *The lost villages of England* (1954; 2nd edn, Gloucester, 1983).

Beresford, M., 'A review of historical research', in M. Beresford and J.G. Hurst (eds), *Deserted medieval villages: studies* (London, 1971), pp. 3–75.

Beresford, M.W., 'Glebe terriers and open field Leicestershire', *Transactions of the Leicestershire Archaeological and Historical Society*, 24 (1948), pp. 77–126.

Bettey, J., 'Downlands', in J. Thirsk (ed.), *Rural England: an illustrated history of the landscape* (Oxford, 2002), pp. 27–49.

Brassley, P., *The agricultural economy of Northumberland and Durham in the period 1640–1750* (London, 1985).

Brassley, P., 'Land drainage', in J. Thirsk, J. (ed.), *The agrarian history of England and Wales, volume VII 1850–1914* (Cambridge, 2000), pp. 514–21.

Brenner, R., 'Agrarian class structure and economic development in pre-industrial Europe', in T.H. Aston and C.H.E. Philpin (eds), *The Brenner debate: agrarian class structure in pre-industrial Europe* (Cambridge, 1987), pp. 10–63.

Broad, J., 'Understanding village desertion in the seventeenth and eighteenth centuries', in C. Dyer and R.L.C. Jones (eds), *Deserted villages revisited* (Hatfield, 2010), pp. 121–39.

Brockett, J.T. *A glossary of north country words in use, with their etymology and affinity to other languages and occasional notices of local customs and popular superstitions* (Newcastle-Upon-Tyne, 1829).

Brown, D., 'Reassessing the influence of the aristocratic improver: the example of the fifth duke of Bedford (1765–1802)', *Agricultural History Review*, 47 (1999), pp. 182–95.

Brown, G., 'Post-enclosure farmsteads on Salisbury Plain: a preliminary discussion', in P. Pattison, D. Field and S. Ainsworth (eds), *Patterns of the past: essays in landscape archaeology for Christopher Taylor* (Oxford, 1999), pp. 121–8.

Butler, J.E., *Memoir of John Grey of Dilston* (Edinburgh, 1869).

Butlin, R.A., 'Field systems of Northumberland and Durham', in A.R.H. Baker and R.A. Butlin (eds), *Studies of field systems in the British Isles* (Cambridge, 1973), pp. 93–144.

Carter, S., Tipping, R., Davidson, D., Long, D. and Tyler, A., 'A multiproxy approach to the function of post-medieval ridge-and-furrow cultivation in upland northern Britain', *The Holocene*, 7 (1997), pp. 447–56.

Cary, J., *New maps of England and Wales with part of Scotland* (London, 1793).

Chambers, J.D. and Mingay, G.E., *The agricultural revolution 1750–1880* (London, 1966).

Chapman, J. and Seeliger, S., *Enclosure, environment and landscape* (London, 2001).

Clay, C., 'Landlords and estate management in England', in J. Thirsk (ed.), *The agrarian history of England and Wales*, Vol. V (Cambridge, 1985), pp. 119–251.

Colbeck, T.I., 'On the agriculture of Northumberland', *Journal of the Royal Agricultural Society of England*, 8 (1847), pp. 422–37.

Colyer, R.J., 'Some aspects of land occupation in nineteenth-century Cardiganshire', *Transactions of the Honourable Society of Cymmrodorion* (1981), pp. 79–97.

Cook, H. and Williamson, T. (eds), *Water management in the English Landscape* (Edinburgh, 1999).

Crust, L., 'William Paddison: marsh farmer and survivor of the agricultural depression, 1873–96', *Agricultural History Review*, 43 (1995), pp. 193–204.

Dixon, P.J., 'The deserted villages of Northumberland: a settlement history from the twelfth to the nineteenth century', PhD thesis (University of Wales, 1984).

Dodgshon, R.A., 'Land improvement in Scottish farming: marl and lime in Roxburghshire and Berwickshire in the eighteenth century', *Agricultural History Review*, 26 (1978), pp. 1–14.

Durham University Library, *Catalogue of Howard Family Papers relating to Cumberland* (2009) <http://endure.dur.ac.uk:8080/fedora/get/UkDhU:EADCatalogue.0137/PDF>, accessed 11 November 2012.

Durham University Library, *Catalogue of the estate records of the Earls Grey* (2009) <http://endure.dur.ac.uk:8080/fedora/get/UkDhU:EADCatalogue.0137/PDF>, accessed 11 November 2012.

Durham University Library, *Catalogue of the papers of Miss Elizabeth Mary Copley and some other Copley papers* (2009) <http://endure.dur.ac.uk:8080/fedora/get/UkDhU:EADCatalogue.0137/PDF>, accessed 30 July 2013.

Dyer, C., 'Conflict in the landscape: the enclosure movement in England 1220–1349', *Landscape History*, 28 (2006), pp. 21–33.

English, B., *The great landowners of East Yorkshire* (London, 1990).

English, B., 'Patterns of estate management in East Yorkshire, c.1840–c.1880', *Agricultural History Review*, 32 (1984), pp. 29–48.

Evans, D.H., Jarrett, M.G. and Wrathmell, S., 'The deserted village of West Whelpington, Northumberland: third report, part two', *Archaeologia Aeliana*, 16 (1988), pp. 139–92.

Farnworth, J., *The Massey legacy: a product and company review of Massey, Harris, Massey-Harris, Ferguson and Massey Ferguson* (Ipswich, 1997).

Farrant, S., 'The management of four estates in the Lower Ouse Valley, Sussex, and agricultural change, 1840–1920', *Southern History*, 1 (1979), pp. 155–70.

Gent, D., 'The seventh earl of Carlisle and the Castle Howard estate: whiggery, religion and improvement, 1830–1864', *Yorkshire Archaeological Journal*, 82 (2010), pp. 315–41.

Gerrard, C.M., 'A rural landscape explored: people, settlement and land-use at Shapwick from prehistory to the present day', in C.M. Gerrard with M. Aston (eds), *The Shapwick Project, Somerset: a rural landscape explored* (Leeds, 2007), pp. 937–1012.

Gerrard, C.M. and Aston, M.A., *Interpreting the English village: landscape and community at Shapwick, Somerset* (Oxford, 2013).

Ginter, D.E., 'Measuring the decline of the small landowner', in B.A. Holderness and M.E. Turner (eds), *Land, labour and agriculture 1700–1920: essays for Gordon Mingay* (London: 1991), pp. 27–48.

Grey, J., 'A view of the past and present state of agriculture in Northumberland', *Journal of the Royal Agricultural Society of England*, 2 (1841), pp. 151–92.

Grigg, D., *The agricultural revolution in south Lincolnshire* (Cambridge, 1966).

Grigg, D., 'Farm size in England and Wales, from early Victorian times to the present', *Agricultural History Review*, 35 (1987), pp. 179–89.

Hammond, J.L. and Hammond, B., *The village labourer 1760–1832: a study of the government of England before the Reform Bill* (1911; Stroud, 1995).

Harrison, J.G., 'East Flanders Moss, Perthshire: a documentary study', *Landscape History*, 30 (2008), pp. 5–19.

Harrison, S., Pile, S. and Thrift, N. (eds), *Patterned ground: entanglements of nature and culture* (London, 2004).

Harvey, N., *A history of farm buildings in England and Wales* (Newton Abbot, 1970).

Hinchcliffe, S., 'Working with multiples: a non-representational approach to environmental issues', in B. Anderson and P. Harrison (eds), *Taking place: non-representational theories and geography* (Farnham, 2010), pp. 303–20.

Hodder, I., *Reading the past: current approaches to interpretation in archaeology* (1986; 2nd edn, Cambridge, 2001).

Hodgson, R.I., 'The enclosure of open fields and extinction of common rights in England c.1600–1750', in H. Fox and R. Butlin (eds), *Change in the countryside essays on rural England 1500–1900* (London, 1979), pp. 83–102.

Holmes, H., 'The circulation of Scottish agricultural books during the eighteenth century', *Agricultural History Review*, 54 (2006), pp. 45–78.

Hoskins, W.G., *The making of the English landscape* (London, 1955).

Hoskins, W.G., *The midland peasant: the economic and social history of a Leicestershire village* (1957; 2nd edn, London, 1965).

Hughes, E., *North country life in the eighteenth century: the north-east 1700–1750* (Oxford, 1952).

Hunt, E.H. and Pam, S.J., 'Prices and structural response in English agriculture, 1873–1896', *The Economic History Review*, 50 (1997), pp. 477–505.

John, A.H., 'The course of agricultural change 1660–1760', in L.S. Pressnell (ed.), *Studies in the industrial revolution: presented to T.S. Ashton* (London, 1960), pp. 125–55.

Johnson, M., *An archaeology of capitalism* (Oxford, 1996).

Johnstone, M., 'Farm rents and improvement: East Lothian and Lanarkshire, 1670–1830', *Agricultural History Review*, 57 (2009), pp. 37–57.

Jones, E.L., 'Eighteenth-century changes in Hampshire chalkland farming', *Agricultural History Review*, 8 (1960), pp. 5–19.

Kain, R.J.P., Chapman, J. and Oliver, R.R., *The enclosure maps of England and Wales 1595–1918* (Cambridge, 2004).

Kerridge, E., *The agricultural revolution* (London, 1967).

Lambert, A., 'Grey, Sir Frederick William (1805–1878)', in *Oxford dictionary of national biography* (online edn, Oxford, 2004) <http://www.oxforddnb.com/view/article/50204>, accessed 1 July 2013.

Latour, B., *Reassembling the social: an introduction to actor-network theory* (2005; pbk edn, Oxford, 2007).

Latour, B., *We have never been modern* (Cambridge, MA, 1993).

Law, J., 'And if the global were small and non-coherent? Method, complexity and the baroque', *Environment and Planning D: Society and Space*, 22 (2004), pp. 13–26.

Law, J., 'Making a mess with method' (Lancaster, 2003) <http://www.lancs.ac.uk/fass/sociology/research/publications/papers/law-making-a-mess-with-method.pdf>, accessed 30 June 2013.

Law, J., *Organising modernity* (Oxford, 1994).

McCloskey, D.N., 'English open fields as behaviour towards risk', *Research in Economic History*, 1 (1976), pp. 123–60.

MacDonald, S., 'The diffusion of knowledge among Northumberland farmers, 1780–1815', *Agricultural History Review*, 27 (1979), pp. 30–39.

MacDonald, S., 'The model farm', in G.E. Mingay (ed.), *The Victorian countryside* (London, 1981), pp. 214–26.

Marshall, W., *On the landed property of England* (London, 1804)

Mingay, G.E., *Parliamentary enclosure in England: an introduction to its causes, incidence and impact* (London, 1997).

Mingay, G.E., 'The size of farms in the eighteenth century', *Economic History Review*, 14 (1962), pp. 469–88.

Mol, A., *The body multiple: ontology in medical practice* (Durham, NC, 2002).

Mol, A. and Law, J., 'Regions networks and fluids: anemia and social topology', *Social Studies of Science*, 24 (1994), pp. 641–71.

Moore, D.C., 'The Corn Laws and high farming', *Economic History Review*, 18 (1965), pp. 544–61.

Moore-Colyer, R., 'Land and people in Northamptonshire: Great Oakley, c.1750–1850', *Agricultural History Review*, 45 (1997), pp. 149–64.

Newton, R., *The Northumberland landscape* (London, 1972).

O'Donnell, R.P. 'Landscape agency and enclosure: transformations in the rural landscape of north-east England', PhD thesis (University of Durham, 2014).

O'Donnell, R.P., 'Conflict, agreement and landscape change: methods of enclosure of the northern English countryside', *Journal of Historical Geography*, 30 (2013), pp. 1–13.

O'Donnell, R.P., 'The creation of ring-fence farms: some observations from Northumberland', *Agricultural History Review*, 63 (2015), pp.39–59.

Overton, M., 'Agricultural revolution? Development of the agrarian economy in early-modern England', in A.R.H. Baker and D. Gregory (eds), *Explorations in historical geography: interpretive essays* (Cambridge, 1984), pp. 118–39.

Overton, M., *Agricultural revolution in England: the transformation of the agrarian economy 1500–1850* (Cambridge, 1996).

Overton, M., 'Re-establishing the agricultural revolution', *Agricultural History Review*, 44 (1996), pp. 1–20.

Parry, M.L., 'Secular climate change and marginal agriculture', *Transactions of the Institute of British Geographers*, 64 (1975), pp. 1–13.

Petts, D. and Gerrard, C.M., *Shared visions: the North East Regional Research Framework for the Historic Environment* (Durham, 2006).

Pevsner, N. and Richmond, I.A., *The buildings of England: Northumberland* (1957; 5th edn, London, 1987).

Philips, A.D.M., *The underdraining of farmland in England during the nineteenth century* (Cambridge, 1989).

Prince, H.C., 'The changing rural landscape', in G.E. Mingay (ed.), *The agrarian history of England and Wales*, Vol. VI (Cambridge, 1989), pp. 7–83.

Prothero, R.E., *English farming past and present* (1912; 6th edn, London, 1961).

Russell, N., *Like engend'ring like: heredity and animal breeding in early modern England* (Cambridge, 1986).

Searl, C.E., 'Customary tenants and the enclosure of the Cumbrian commons', *Northern History*, 29 (1993), pp. 126–53.

Searl, G.R., *The Liberal Party: triumph and disintegration 1886–1929* (Basingstoke, 1992).

Sheppard, J.A., 'Small farms in a Sussex weald parish 1800–1860', *Agricultural History Review*, 40 (1992), pp. 127–41.

Short, B., 'The turnover of tenants on the Ashburnham estate, 1830–1850', *Sussex Archaeological Collections*, 113 (1976), pp. 157–74.

Smith, E.A., *Lord Grey 1764–1845* (Oxford, 1990).

Stephens, T. (ed.), *The register of baptisms, marriages and burials solemnized in the ancient parish in the ancient parish church of Elsdon, in the county of Northumberland* (Newcastle-upon-Tyne, 1903).

Straughton, E.A., *Common grazing in the northern English uplands, 1800–1965: a history of national policy and local practice with special attention to the case of Cumbria* (Lampeter, 2008).

Tarlow, S., *The archaeology of improvement in Britain 1750–1850* (Cambridge, 2007).

Tate, W.E., *A domesday of English enclosure acts and awards* (Reading, 1978).

Thirsk, J., *Alternative agriculture: a history from the Black Death to the present day* (Oxford, 1997).

Thirsk, J., 'Enclosing and engrossing', in J. Thirsk (ed.), *The agrarian history of England and Wales*, Vol. IV (Cambridge, 1967), pp. 200–56.

Thompson, F.M.L., 'Life after death: how successful nineteenth-century businessmen disposed of their fortunes', *Economic History Review*, 43 (1990), pp. 40–61.

Thompson, F.M.L., 'The second agricultural revolution, 1815–1880', *Economic History Review*, 21 (1968), pp. 62–77.

Turner, M.E., *Enclosures in Britain 1750–1830* (London, 1984).

Turner, M.E., *English parliamentary enclosure: its historical geography and economic history* (Folkestone, 1980).

Upex, S., 'A classification of ridge-and-furrow by an analysis of cross-profiles', *Landscape History*, 26 (2004), pp. 59–75.

Vickers, K.H., *A history of Northumberland*, Vol. XI (Newcastle-upon-Tyne, 1922).

Wade-Martins, S., *The English model farm: building the agricultural ideal, 1700–1914* (Oxford, 2002).

Wade-Martins, S. and Williamson, T., 'The development of the lease and its role in agricultural improvement in East Anglia, 1660–1870', *Agricultural History Review*, 46 (1998), pp. 127–41.

Whyte, I., 'The costs of parliamentary enclosure in an upland setting: south and east Cumbria 1760–1860', *Northern History*, 43 (2006), pp. 97–115.

Whyte, I., 'Wild, barren and frightful: parliamentary enclosure in an upland county, Westmorland 1767–1890', *Rural History*, 14 (2003), pp. 21–38.

Williamson, T., '"At pleasure's lordly call": the archaeology of emparked settlements', in C. Dyer and R.L.C. Jones (eds), *Deserted villages revisited* (Hatfield, 2010), pp. 162–81.

Williamson, T., *Sandlands: the Suffolk coast and heaths* (Macclesfield, 2005).

Williamson, T., *The transformation of rural England: farming and the landscape 1700–1870* (Exeter, 2002).

Wilson, J.M., *The rural cyclopedia*, Vol. IV (London, 1849).

Wittering, S.A., *Ecology and enclosure: the effect of enclosure on society, farming and the environment in south Cambridgeshire, 1798–1850* (Oxford, 2013).

Wordie, J.R., 'Social change on the Leveson-Gower estates, 1714–1832', *Economic History Review*, 27 (1974), pp. 593–609.

Wrathmell, S., 'Deserted and shrunken villages in southern Northumberland from the twelfth to the twentieth centuries', PhD thesis (University of Wales, 1975).

Wrathmell, S., 'Village depopulation in the 17th and 18th centuries: examples from Northumberland', *Post-Medieval Archaeology*, 14 (1980), pp. 113–26.

Wykes, D.L., 'Robert Bakewell (1725–1795) of Dishley: farmer and livestock improver', *Agricultural History Review*, 52 (2004), pp. 38–55.

Wylie, J., *Landscape* (London, 2007).

Yelling, J.A., *Common field and enclosure in England 1450–1850* (London, 1977).

Young, A., *A six months tour through the north of England* (London, 1771).

Young, A., *A six weeks tour through the southern counties of England and Wales* (Edinburgh, 1772).

Index